Legacy of Lace

Identifying, Collecting, and Preserving American Lace

Kathleen Warnick and Shirley Nilsson

Crown Publishers, Inc., New York

A Solstice Press Book

Produced at North Country Book Express, Inc. by Karla Fromm,
Beth Goodnight, Kristin Mullally, Melissa Rockwood, and Mary Schierman
under the direction of Ivar Nelson and Patricia Hart.

Design by Karla Fromm. Illustrations by Melissa Rockwood.
Photos by Don Hamilton and Larry Cobb.

Published by Crown Publishers, Inc., 225 Park Avenue South, New York,
New York 10003, and represented in Canada by the Canadian MANDA Group

CROWN is a trademark of Crown Publishers, Inc.

Manufactured in the United States of America

Library of Congress Cataloging-in-Publication Data

Warnick, Kathleen.
    Legacy of lace: Identifying, collecting, and preserving American lace / by
Kathleen Warnick and Shirley Nilsson.
        p.   cm.
        Bibliography: p.
        Includes index.
        1. Lace and lacemaking—United States—Collectors and collecting.
    2. Lace and lacemaking—Conservation and restoration—United States.
    I. Nilsson, Shirley. II. Title.
    NK9412.W37   1988
    746.2'2'0973—dc19   87-37959
    ISBN 0-517-56899-3   CIP

10 9 8 7 6 5 4 3 2 1

First Edition

Contents

Acknowledgments

The authors gratefully acknowledge the encouragement and good advice received from the experts who reviewed the draft of this book: Muriel M. Mitchell, Burnaby, B.C., lace identification consultant; Kathe Kliot, Berkeley, CA, owner of LACIS Antique Lace and Textile Center; Leila Old, Moscow, ID, Professor Emerita, Home Economics, University of Idaho; Glenda Pifer, Washington, D.C., National Extension Program Leader; Mary C. Saylor, University Park, PA, Extension Related Arts Specialist; and Marian Simms, Elko, B.C., "lace lady" at Fort Steele historical museum.

We express our appreciation to the Leila Old Historic Costume Collection from which we borrowed dress models and the Irish crochet blouse, child's dress trimmed with tatting, Hardanger skirt, and accessories to photograph, and to the Latah County Historical Society, Moscow, Idaho, for photographs. Interior photographs facing the beginning of each chapter showing how lace was used in the early 1900s were taken at the Campbell House of the Eastern Washington Historical Society and the Patsy Clark restaurant in Spokane, Washington.

We are particularly thankful to family members in older generations who endowed us with interest in heritage textile crafts and the core of our lace collections. We thank all our friends and relatives who have given us pieces of lace (with special thanks to the Margaret Ritchie and Alma Lauder Keeling estates) or loaned us pieces to photograph, and to everyone who has expressed enthusiasm for this project.

The types of lace shown in the room scenes that introduce the major sections of the text are listed on the last page.

Introduction to Lace Identification

In a box from grandmother's attic, in an old trunk, or at a rummage sale, you find a piece of filigree threadwork. Is it lace? How was it made?

This book will help you identify the pieces of lace and lacy embroidery from your trunks, attics, and linen closets, and those you see at rummage sales, in antique shops, or in museums and historic collections. The emphasis is on the types of lace that have been popular in America during the past one hundred years.

This book also reviews the history of lace. Practical suggestions on how old laces and other fabrics should be preserved and ideas about how old and new laces can be used today are included.

The laces described are mainly the kinds our grandmothers and great-grandmothers made or purchased to decorate their clothing or homes, acquired as souvenirs, and received as gifts. Relatively little is included about the many varieties of bobbin lace and needle lace, because there are a number of books devoted to these laces. Differentiating among the various bobbin laces and needle laces, which most of us will see only in special collections, is beyond the scope of this book. What this book will do is help you identify by their basic construction techniques the pieces of lace and lacy embroidery which you are most likely to find. A few techniques, such as sprang, that are not well known today are included to round out the historical development of lace.

The best way to identify a piece of lace is to understand the ways the threads are manipulated to make different types of lace, and to be familiar with patterns characteristic of each type. This book illustrates how different types of lace are made and shows construction details to look for. Typical pieces are pictured.

We define *lace* as a "decorative openwork fabric with a design of spaces and denser areas formed by manipulating threads." Using this general definition of lace, we have not been concerned with establishing a difference between lace and openwork embroidery. The definitions of *lace* and *embroidery* overlap. *Embroidery* includes any decorative stitch on a fabric foundation; it can decorate a surface, trim an edge, or create a pattern of holes in a fabric. We have also included some techniques which usually produce articles too heavy to be thought of as being "lacy," but which are "decorative openwork fabrics."

Classifying lace by construction method

Looping

Bringing loops of thread through previously formed loops

Includes: Crochet, hairpin lace, broomstick lace, knitting

Knotting

Tying two or more threads together

Includes: Netting, knotted lace (Armenian lace), macrame, waffle work, tatting

Crossing

Passing threads over and under one another by twisting, braiding, and weaving

Includes: Sprang, weaving, interlacing, bobbin lace

Needlework

Making stitches with a threaded needle

Includes: Needlework on net, needlework on woven fabric, needle lace, Tenerife lace, Battenberg lace

There are a bewildering number of kinds of lace. After much consideration, we determined that the identification process could be simplified by dividing the lacemaking techniques into four major classifications based on the way threads are manipulated to make the lace. These are listed at left.

The same basic thread manipulations are used for making lace by hand and by machine. Machine-made laces are discussed following the sections on handmade laces.

An Identification Key illustrating the major kinds of lace in each of the classifications of lacemaking techniques begins on page 167. Study the piece of lace you wish to identify, over a contrasting background with good light, using a magnifying glass if the lace was made with fine thread. Try to determine if it was made by looping, knotting, crossing the threads, or needlework. Compare it with typical examples pictured in the Key and then refer to the sections in the text which give detailed information.

There are many variations within each of the basic techniques, but if you can tell how the threads were manipulated to form the lace, you will have a general idea what kind of lace you have.

Of course, any classification system results in some items which would fit equally well in more than one group, and some which don't fit well in any group. For example, knotted lace (Armenian lace) could be classified either as knotting or needlework, because it is made by tying knots with a needle. Laces made by incorporating novelty tapes and cords with crochet, tatting, and needlework have been put in a separate classification.

Two or more lacemaking techniques are often combined in a single article. For example, a tablecloth may have a design in cutwork embroidery, borders of drawnwork, and a bobbin lace edging. A knitted doily may be finished with one or more rows of crochet. Bobbin lace motifs may be appliquéd to machine-made net with special features added with needle lace stitches. Study each piece carefully to learn all you can about it.

To understand how threads are manipulated to make laces, watch people making lace by various techniques, and try the techniques yourself. Study as many examples as you can find to see how different sizes of thread and tools, and various degrees of skill in the craft, produce different effects.

The various types of lace have been called many names, and the same names have been used for different laces at other times and at other places. For example, the beautiful sixteenth and seventeenth-century laces made with a needle were called "point lace" from the French word for stitch. Later any fine lace made with needles or bobbins was called "point lace." In the late nineteenth century laces made with machine-made tapes and needlework to imitate the early Italian laces were called "point lace," and so were some machine-made laces. The term "needlepoint" is now used in Britain and other countries to designate laces made with a needle using variations of the buttonhole stitch (like the old Italian laces). However, in the United States, "needlepoint" is a type of wool embroidery on canvas, so the term "needle lace" is used. Even this name can be confusing—in an Oriental import shop a knitted doily was identified as "needle lace." (Just different kinds of needles!) The word "lace" itself has different meanings—a shoe lace is not a decorative openwork fabric.

Perhaps the most confusing name for lace is "Brussels," because it has been applied to bobbin lace, needle lace, appliqué on net, Battenberg lace, and several types of machine made laces. Place names have been given to laces because the lace was made in that locality, or because it bears a real or imagined resemblance to some lace which was made there, but the name often gives us very little information about what type of lace the piece actually is.

Unfortunately, many of the labels on lacy articles we see in shops and museums don't give us information which will help us learn to identify laces. Some don't tell us anything we didn't already know—"lace trimmed handkerchief," "lace doily," or simply "lace." Some labels use names which by themselves can indicate a number of types of lace—is a piece labeled "Brussels lace" bobbin lace, needle lace, or some other type? Some labels are just plain wrong—a bobbin lace mat purchased in an antique shop was labeled "Irish croquet"!

In this book, laces are classified by their basic construction technique, with their most commonly used names.

"Is it *real* lace?" The answer to this frequently asked question depends on your definition of "lace." Some authorities state that only needle lace and bobbin lace are "real" or "true" laces, and all others are imitations. However, netting, net darning, sprang, macrame, and openwork embroidery are all older techniques for making lacy fabrics than needle lace and bobbin lace, and therefore could not have been developed to imitate them. It is true that crochet was developed to imitate the more time-consuming needle lace, but crocheters soon found that they could produce designs and effects not possible with other techniques, so crocheting became a lacemaking technique in its own right.

Many people consider handmade lace to be "real" and machine-made lace to be "imitation," but this distinction also runs into problems. Lace is a "decorative openwork fabric with a design of spaces and denser areas formed by manipulating threads." Paper or plastic doilies and tablecloths which have lacy designs cut, stamped or printed on them do not meet this definition and are imitation lace—the lacy designs have not been made by manipulating threads. Handmade and machine-made laces do meet the definition. Some machine-made laces are "lacier" and more beautiful than some handmade ones, and are more appropriate for some uses. Some machine-made reproductions are so exact that it is difficult to determine whether some pieces of lace were made by machine or by hand. Some laces are made by combining machine-made parts (such as tapes or net) with handwork. In countries where the sale of "handmade lace" is an important industry, laws prescribe the amount of handwork which must be included in making a piece of lace in order for it to be labeled "handmade."

You don't need to look very far to find examples of many kinds of lace. Most of the examples in this book were in the "family accumulations" of the authors, gifts from friends who knew we were interested in lace, and samples we made to try out lace-making techniques. Some pieces were purchased at rummage sales, auctions, and antique shops to round out our collections.

Lace has special enchantment, and treasured articles of clothing, accessories, and household linens with lace on them provide a link with the past. We feel closer to our heritage when we enjoy things earlier generations enjoyed and know how their handcrafted articles were made. In our highly mechanized, computerized society, as we try to balance "high tech" with "high touch," there is new appreciation for the handcrafts that delighted our grandparents and their grandparents.

History

Lace is a decorative openwork fabric with a design of open spaces and denser areas formed by manipulating threads. The derivation of the word tells something of the history of lacemaking and the appeal of lace—the word *lace* comes from two related Latin words meaning *snare* and *to entice*. Netted lace developed from the crude snares tied by our ancient ancestors.

Lacemaking shares the heritage of other textiles. Twisting two vines together may have been man's first step toward forming a textile; fish and animal snares and game bags made of knotted reeds, vines, and grasses were among the earliest of human inventions and have been found in most primitive cultures. Gradually it was learned that short fibers could be twisted together to make longer and stronger threads and that these could be knotted, crossed, or looped together to form textiles. As civilizations advanced, fibers were used for decorative as well as utilitarian purposes.

The basic techniques of manipulating threads were refined to make early forms of lace. Because fibers are perishable, historians have had few actual samples from early civilizations to study, but ancient tombs yield some textile products, tools used to make them, and pictures and carvings showing textiles in use.

Ancient Egyptian art depicts hair nets as early as 2130 B.C. Costumes on carvings from Babylon and Assyria appear to include ornamental knotting and braiding. Lacy fabrics were used in early biblical times.

Netted laces were used to decorate church and household textiles in Europe by the thirteenth century, and fancy braids were used for trim all through the Middle Ages. Bobbin lace and needle lace developed in Europe in the 1400s; the earliest definite references to bobbin lace are in pictures and inventories of the great Italian families from 1476 on. Needle lace was made in the latter part of the fifteenth century in Venice. Lacemaking was widespread in Europe by the time Columbus sailed to America.

Many countries claim that lacemaking originated in their area and have charming legends supporting their claims. A Venetian legend tells that lace was invented by a lovesick girl who spent hours gazing at a piece of coral her sailor had given her and then imitated its slender and intricate branches with a mazy web of linen thread. Belgium has a romantic story that a knight going on

Latah County Historical Society

5

a Crusade left his lady a rose. Every time a petal began to fall apart, she sewed it together. Eventually the original rose was all gone and she had a needle-made one in its place. Another Belgian legend tells the origin of bobbin lace. A maiden prayed to the Madonna for a miracle so she could get the money to buy medicine for her widowed mother. As she sat praying in a garden, a perfect spider web fell on her dark apron. She worked and worked trying to copy the delicate pattern, but her threads tangled until her lover cut pieces of twigs on which she wound the threads. She taught nuns and novices in the convent to make the lace, which was sold to the Court and the Church.

It is difficult for us to imagine now the importance of lace during the sixteenth, seventeenth, and eighteenth centuries in Europe. Today we think of lace as a lovely but somewhat frivolous extra, and very feminine, though for hundreds of years in Europe, lace was extensively worn by men as well as by women of the aristocracy. Large quantities of lace were used in churches for altar cloths and communion linens and in the vestments worn by church officials. These vestments were elaborate articles of ceremonial attire, varying with the rank of the wearer and the rite being celebrated.

Laces were prized possessions to be itemized in any inventory of one's assets. Lace was a status symbol. Lace was used in household decoration and in women's clothing and was also worn by men as instep rosettes, boot-top flounces, hat ornaments, collars and cuffs, and decorations on coats, nightshirts, and other garments.

One reason lace became so popular in Europe was that severe laws and taxes repressed the wearing of gold, silver, jewels, and silk. Lace—a product of plain white thread—provided the chance to evade those laws and gratify the taste for luxury and artistic beauty in dress. Fortunes were spent on lace. In the sixteenth century, during the Reformation, the wearing of lace was condemned by some Protestant leaders because lace "doth neither hide nor heat." Puritan women satisfied their consciences and gratified their taste for lace and embroidery by using subjects associated with the Scriptures. Satirists of the time referred to "religious petticoats" and "historical shirts."

Governments issued edicts and imposed restrictions and taxes in efforts to curtail ruinously extravagant expenditures on costly imported laces and to protect home industry. In the reign of Louis XIV at the beginning of the eighteenth century, the death penalty was imposed on those who attempted to carry lace secrets beyond the borders of France. Importation of foreign lace was prohibited by France and England. This, of course, led to smuggling. The value of the lace well repaid the smugglers' risks and efforts. Ingenious methods were devised. Small quantities of lace were hidden in parasols, books, bakery goods, and on babies. Corpses were dressed in yards and yards of fine lace and the coffins transported across the Channel. After a burial service, the coffins were secretly dug up to retrieve the lace. Some coffins contained no bodies—just lace.

Lacemaking was the main economic support of many communities as a cottage industry, with particular types of lace, patterns, and techniques characteristic of different localities. Nuns in convents made lace and established schools for lacemaking. They would teach children as young as five, and by the time children were ten they were expected to make enough lace to pay their expenses. In lacemaking villages throughout Europe, every house would have one or more persons making lace whenever they were not busy with other work. Women, children, men unable to do more arduous labor, and fishermen beached by heavy weather all made lace.

Periodically, a buyer would come through the countryside and collect the finished pieces, leaving an equivalent amount of thread. It was customary for a lacemaker to make only one kind of lace and to work on only one pattern in order to develop the greatest possible skill and speed. For complicated laces, different workers made different parts of the lace—only flowers or only leaves, for example. These parts were collected by the buyers and taken to other workers who assembled the finished lace and put in the background.

Lace was rarely designed and made by the same person. Patterns were drawn by a designer, then transferred to stiff parchment. These were precious and were carefully guarded by each family and lace district.

Production of special laces required rigorous working conditions. Any form of flame heat could cause soot damage to fine white threads. During the winter in some areas, lace was made in special rooms in cow barns where heat from the animals warmed the air. Some flax was spun into threads so fine they could hardly be seen and had to be manipulated by touch alone. Bright light and dryness weakened threads, so spinning and lacemaking were done in dim, damp rooms. Under these conditions, poor eyesight and lung diseases were common.

Despite what seem to us to have been horrible working conditions, lacemaking was a preferred occupation. A Swiss pattern book published in 1550 stated that women could earn a better living making bobbin lace than with a spindle, shuttle, or anything else. Some laws were passed forbidding the making of lace because of the "servant problem," that is, so many women were making lace that it was hard to get servants. English nuns were warned "not to give to the fair laces time that should be spent in shaping, sewing, and mending church vestments and poor people's clothing."

Making bobbin lace, needle lace, and openwork embroidery were important cottage industries in parts of Britain, France, the Low Countries, Switzerland, and Italy. All over Europe, these and other kinds of lace were also made for personal use and for the churches. Certain types and patterns were characteristic of particular areas and were important parts of folk costumes and customs.

Colonists who came to America brought with them the skills they had learned in their home countries. Frontier life was rigorous, but to the extent that time and materials were available, colonial homemakers embellished their household articles and clothing with lace and openwork embroidery. These were not merely decorative—they were often used to refurbish old garments or to combine pieces of worn articles into something serviceable and attractive. Women shared their skills with their neighbors, so many ethnic and national traditions contributed to the richness and diversity of American needlecrafts.

Emigrants who had made their living by lacemaking found no comparable cottage industry in America. There was no network of middlemen supplying the necessary thread and taking the finished lace to the purchasers. Because communications and travel were difficult while America was being settled, the well-to-do who could afford to purchase lace could obtain it more easily from their established suppliers in Europe.

A notable exception to the general lack of lacemaking cottage industries was at Ipswich, Massachusetts, about twenty miles north of Boston, which was settled by lacemakers from Ipswich in the English Midlands. A 1790 survey by Alexander Hamilton reported over 600 lacemakers in that area.

As the frontier moved west, life became easier in the towns and cities along the Atlantic coast. More women had time to do decorative handwork. Newspapers from the early 1700s on carried advertisements offering instruction in various types of needlework and lacemaking, as well as for the necessary supplies and equipment.

The industrial revolution had profound effects on lacemaking in the nineteenth century. Machines were developed in England that could produce lace much cheaper than hand-workers could. When the advantages of lace machines became recognized, England tried to prevent their exportation, but machines were smuggled to France and other countries. In 1818 the essential parts of the first lacemaking machine to reach America arrived in Massachusetts concealed in tubs of butter.

As improved machines made increasingly accurate reproductions of handmade lace, lacemaking as a cottage industry died out. But at the same time, the industrial revolution produced a leisured middle class in Europe and America for whom handwork was a pleasurable pastime. Spinning machines took over the laborious chore of spinning thread by hand, and a wide variety of threads became readily available. Ladies enthusiastically tried the traditional lacemaking techniques and experimented with new ways to make lacy fabrics.

By the middle of the 1800s, instructions for openwork embroidery and lacemaking were being published in American magazines and booklets, so women all over the country were working on the same techniques and patterns.

During the Victorian era, in America as in Europe, styles of clothing and home furnishings called for lavish amounts of lace. Lacemaking was a "gentle art," at which well-to-do women and girls spent their leisure time. The objects created by the busy work for idle hands were prominently displayed in homes. Fringes fell from the edges of pianos, mantels, shelves, and tables. Curtains were made of lace or were lace-trimmed, as were tablecloths, bed curtains, coverlets, and bed skirts. Arms and headrests of upholstered furniture were protected with decorative lace antimacassars. Dark, highly polished wooden surfaces were protected by lace or lace-edged cloths, scarves, and runners. Doilies covered everything, both as washable protectors and as ways to show off accomplishments in the gentle arts. Well-bred young ladies were expected to create hope chests of usable household items to demonstrate their competence in needlecraft skills and to provide lovely useful items for their new homes.

Lace was also made by women who had hardly any leisure time at all. We look at the beautiful pieces of lace made by women who had no household help and none of the modern laborsaving devices and marvel that they found the time and energy to make them. After days of monotonous toil, carrying water, cooking on a wood stove, scrubbing clothes on a washboard, ironing with a sadiron, sewing and mending the family's clothes, they created delicate beauty with plain thread by candle and lamp light. By their own skill, they were able to bring beauty into their lives. The design, carefully worked out, represented perfection in a very imperfect world. Lacemaking and other forms of fancywork offered women who had more skill than money a chance to "keep up with the Joneses" in one area. Handwork was a rewarding form of relaxation—even a few moments crocheting would take the worker a step toward completing a collar or a tablecloth, whereas cooking and scrubbing were never finished.

In the early 1900s, fashions swung toward simplicity. The lavish use of lace in home decoration was no longer stylish. Inexpensive machine-made lace insertions and edgings were available as simple trim on women's and girls' underwear, blouses, and summer dresses. Many of the techniques of making lace by hand became almost lost arts.

Since the 1960s there has been a revival of interest in the old lacemaking techniques. Doilies, table linens, and collars, which had been stored away when they went out of style, have been rediscovered and are being appreciated for their beauty and craftsmanship. People searching for their roots find that old lace pieces make them feel closer to previous generations who had treasured the laces and preserved them. By learning to identify different types of lace, we can hope to increase our enjoyment of these old pieces and of pieces made today using the old techniques in traditional and innovative ways.

Latah County Historical Society

Latah County Historical Society

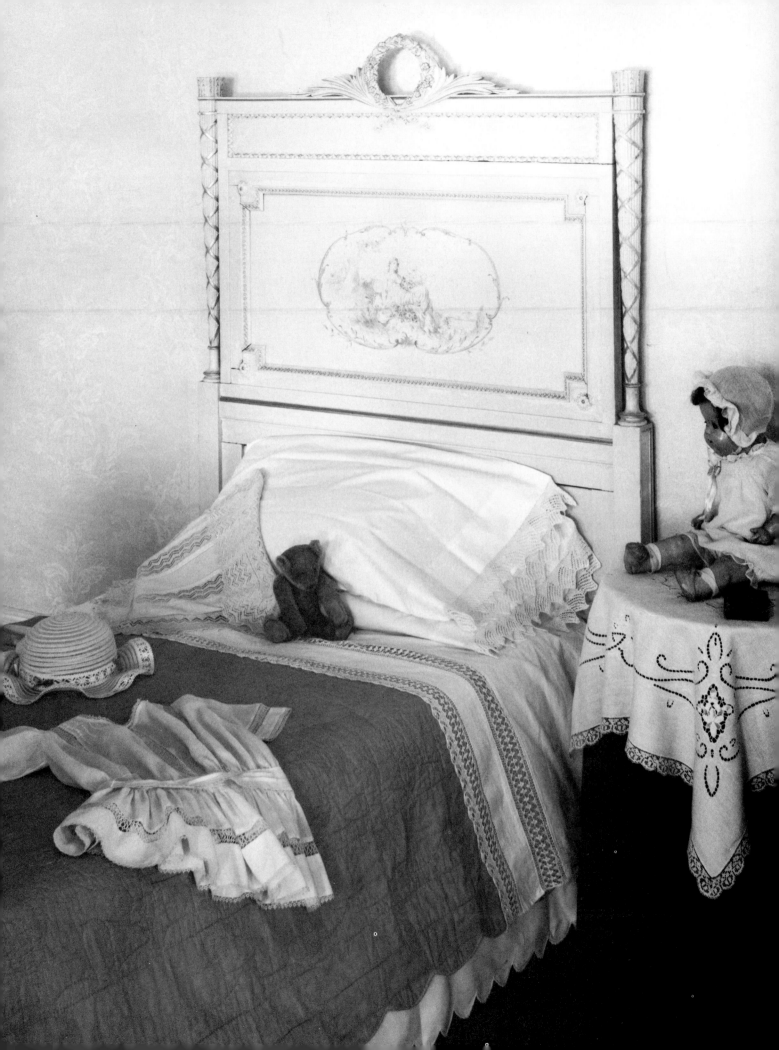

Looping

Bringing loops of thread through previously formed loops

The art of making a fabric by pulling one loop of fiber through another probably developed in many primitive cultures. Someone playing with a fiber by winding it around the fingers found that pulling the adjacent part of the fiber through a loop and repeating the action produced a chain. Then someone found that by folding the end of the chain back and pulling a loop through the chain and through the last loop that a wider strip could be made. Working back and forth along the strip eventually produced a large enough piece of fabric to use as a garment or blanket. If the first and last loops of a short length of chain were joined in a circle, and stitches made round and round, a circular mat or a bowl shape resulted, depending on how many stitches were added as the circumference increased. This process is known as finger crochet.

It is easy to imagine ancient herders plucking wool from sheep or camels, or gathering wool pulled off of bushes, twisting the fibers in their fingers to make thread and looping the thread into a loose fabric as they watched their herds. Later, someone found that a hooked stick could be used instead of fingers to pull the thread through the loops, and the technique we call *crochet* was invented. Eventually it was discovered that the loops could be held on a stick and new loops could be pulled through with another stick, and *knitting* was invented.

Looped fabrics were made in the Near East around 1000 B.C. or earlier. Ancient Pima Indians in Arizona, working with fibers from tree bark, fashioned loose baskets, which they plastered with clay, to use as cooking pots. Shards of these pots show the imprint of looped stitches.

Looping Techniques

Crochet

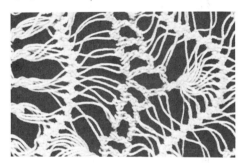

Hairpin Lace

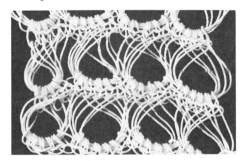

Broomstick Lace

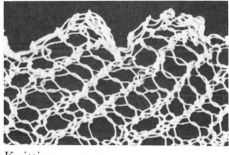

Knitting

Crochet

The type of handmade lace most commonly found in trunks and attics in America is crochet. Crochet is a simple technique, requiring only a hook to loop a continuous thread into a fabric. The word *crochet* comes from the French word *croche,* meaning little hook. Crochet is an extremely versatile technique — the same basic stitches can make dainty handkerchief edgings or heavy rugs. Designs vary from delicate webs to exquisite flowers to solid geometrics.

The earliest surviving examples of lace made with a hook are on a banner from the tomb of a twelfth-century bishop, which is now in a museum in Barcelona, Spain. Some hooked lace was made by nuns in Italy and France from the sixteenth century on, imitating the more time-consuming needle lace and bobbin lace of the time. Contemporary accounts of Queen Elizabeth I's wardrobe include references to caps made of "knot work, worked with

This corset cover from the early 1900s has a crocheted yoke with sleeves.

chain stitch" and "flourished with chain stitch."

Crochet was introduced to Ireland early in the 1800s by French nuns and was developed and popularized in England by Mademoiselle Eleanore Riego de la Branchardière. Born in England, Mademoiselle Riego was the daughter of an Irish mother and a French nobleman. She devoted her life to the study of needlework, developing better methods, improving materials and equipment, and designing new patterns. She published over a hundred books on needlecrafts between 1846 and 1887. Mademoiselle Riego studied old samples of crochet lace at Blackrock Convent in Dublin, worked out methods, wrote instructions, and taught the art to members of the English royal family. In her instructions on crochet, Mademoiselle Riego described the first stitch a beginner must learn as "single crochet or shepherd's knitting," which indicates the close relationship between the basic techniques of knitting and crochet.

Although books with instructions and patterns for crochet had been published in England, crocheted lace did not become widely known until the Irish potato famines of 1846 and subsequent years. Nuns in a convent near Cork and several wealthy Englishwomen started teaching men, women, and children to crochet as a way to make money and stave off starvation. Queen Victoria popularized Irish crocheted lace, and it became the latest vogue in high society all over Europe throughout the latter part of the Victorian era. There was a ready market for the lace because the styles in clothing and household decoration of that period were well suited to crocheted lace.

Crocheting became a popular leisure time hobby, especially in America. *Godey's Lady's Book*, an American magazine for women, started printing lace patterns in 1846. Mrs. Ann S. Stephens, in her book *The Ladies' Complete Guide to Crochet, Fancy Knitting and*

A variation of the popular "pineapple" pattern forms the design of this crocheted tablecloth.

Needlework, published in New York in 1854, urged her readers to recognize crochet as "one of those gentle means by which women are kept feminine and ladylike in this fast age."

Crocheted lace at first imitated the old Italian needle laces. Using fine thread and tiny hooks, the crocheter made each rose and leaf separately, then joined them with a chain stitch mesh. Although this is so time-consuming that few crocheters try to duplicate these patterns today, it was about four times faster than making similar patterns with needles or bobbins. Those who were crocheting as a pastime experimented with new stitches, patterns, and types of thread. Filet crochet, in which solid and open squares create designs imitating the centuries-old net darning ("real filet"), became extremely popular. Patterns were also developed that imitated other lacemaking techniques. Needlecraft magazines from the early 1900s on published instructions for crochet resembling retecilla (needle lace), netting, Armenian lace (knotted lace), Cluny and torchon bobbin lace, and tatting. Most of the patterns, however, were unique to crochet—they created effects that could not be obtained with other lacemaking techniques.

Crocheted lace enjoyed great popularity in America. Rose Wilder Lane in the *Women's Day Book of American Needlework* tells of seeing an exhibit of crocheted articles in the National Museum of Croatia (Yugoslavia) in the 1920s. The curator identified the display as "our collection of the art of the American lace."

Making a crocheted chain.

Below: Basic crochet stitches: single crochet (left), double crochet (center), triple crochet (right).

Bottom: Fans/scallops (left) and clusters (right) made with double crochet stitches.

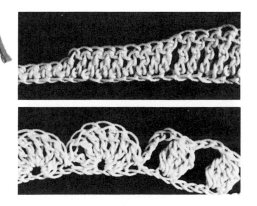

Construction

Crocheting begins with a chain: a loop is made in the thread, the hook goes through the loop, picks up the thread and pulls it through the loop, forming the next loop, and the process is repeated.

In addition to starting a piece of crochet, chains connect solid areas of the design, provide space for additional stitches in the next row, or form a mesh, which is, itself, all or part of the design.

The three stitches most frequently used to make the solid areas of a design are:

1. Single crochet: The hook, holding the loop of the last chain or other stitch, goes through a stitch in the preceding row or chain, picks up the thread and pulls it through; then the thread is picked up by the hook and pulled through both loops on the hook.

2. Double crochet: The thread is wrapped once around the hook before it is inserted in the stitch in the preceding row; the loop is pulled through that stitch, the thread is picked up by the hook and pulled through two of the loops on the hook, then

the thread is again picked up by the hook and pulled through the last two loops on the hook.

3. Triple crochet: Like double crochet, but the thread is wrapped twice around the hook before it is inserted in the stitch in the preceding row; the loops on the hook are worked off two at a time.

Since 1929 crochet patterns in the United States have used the American system of naming crochet stitches. Older publications used the English system, which is still used in Canada and Britain:

American single crochet = English double crochet
American double crochet = English treble crochet
American triple crochet = English double treble crochet

Scallops and fans are formed by making a number of double or triple crochet stitches in the same stitch of the preceding row. Clusters are made the same way except that the last loop of each stitch is kept on the hook until they are all worked off together.

Crocheted edgings usually start with a chain of the desired length to be sewed to the article; however, the first row is sometimes hooked directly into the fabric. Some edgings are crocheted across the width. Articles such as doilies and tablecloths may be started in the center and worked round after round to the final size, or worked from side to side. Many designs are made up of small medallions crocheted or sewed together.

● Distinctive Features

1. Chains

2. Solid areas of single, double, or triple crochet

3. Picots (small loops of chain stitch)

4. Fans and scallops

Crocheted doily with a design of flowers in a chain stitch mesh and a fan border.

Right: Doily with chain stitch mesh and triple crochet leaves and triangles.

Below right: A "pineapple" pattern butterfly on a handkerchief corner.

Above: Sample edging showing how the design is built up with succeeding rows.

Below: Crocheted edgings, ranging from the simple to the complex.

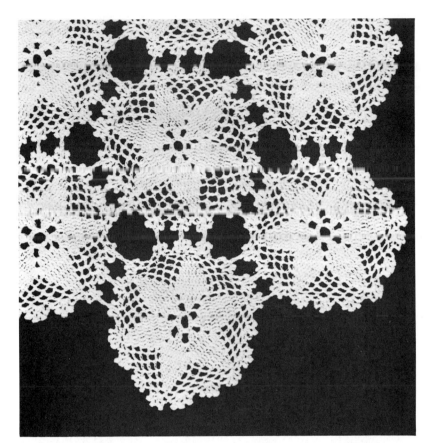

Left: Mat of seven hexagonal medallions.

Below: Mat of twelve round medallions with flowers filling the spaces between the circles.

Irish Crochet

In the middle of the nineteenth century in Ireland, crocheting literally saved thousands of people from starvation during the potato famines. Men, women, and children earned their living crocheting lace. Patterns used then are still called Irish crochet. They typically have three-dimensional flowers and leaves, connected with a background mesh of chain stitches. Kidney-shaped solid areas called beans are often found around flower and leaf motifs. The width and ornateness of a pattern was measured not only in inches but also by the number of beans.

Irish crochet was very popular in America in the late nineteenth and early twentieth centuries. Making very elaborate

Right: This Victorian blouse has an allover design of Irish crochet.

Below: Flower and leaf motifs used in Irish crochet.

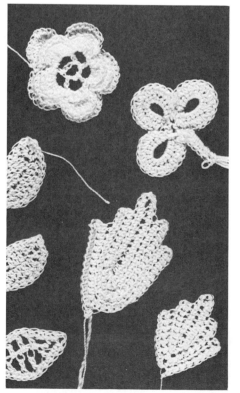

designs in Irish crochet for clothing or household decoration was considered to be worth the effort because the lace could be taken apart by undoing the background, and the motifs could be rearranged to fit new shapes as fashion or function changed.

Construction

In some designs a three-dimensional effect is obtained by making flowers with two or more rows of petals. Leaves are worked with single crochet stitches in the back of the stitches in the preceding row. Since the leaf is turned at the end of each row, the stitches form ridges. Motifs such as flowers, leaves, and stems are often padded by working the crochet stitches over a heavier thread or cord. Heavily padded Irish crochet was hardest to make, but was considered to be the most valuable and durable.

The motifs are made separately and basted to a piece of cloth. A chain stitch mesh background is then worked connecting the motifs. The mesh is usually diamond-shaped, but depending on the space to be filled and the article being made, the mesh may be oblong, circular, hexagonal, or free form.

The mesh often has small loops of chain stitch called picots. Many pieces of Irish crochet have a three-part scallop edging.

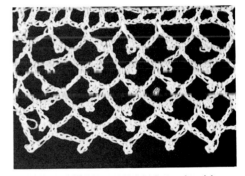

Diamond-shaped chain stitch mesh with picots, frequently used in Irish crochet.

⬤ Distinctive Features

1. Three-dimensional flowers and leaves

2. Chain stitch mesh, often with picots

3. Beans

4. Three-part scallop edging

Irish crochet edging, a three-bean pattern with roses and shamrocks, plain mesh, and three-part scallop edging.

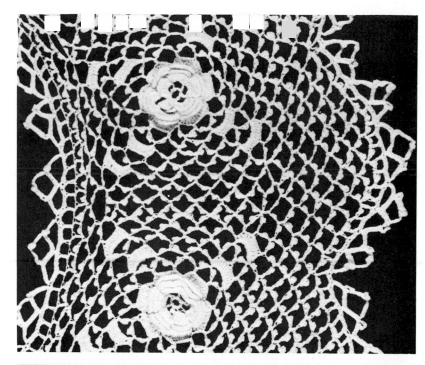

Right: Part of an Irish crochet collar, two-bean pattern with three-dimensional roses, picot mesh, and three-part scallop edging.

Below: An Irish crochet neck piece from the 1920s, with three-dimensional flowers, ribbed leaves, and picot mesh, worked with very fine thread.

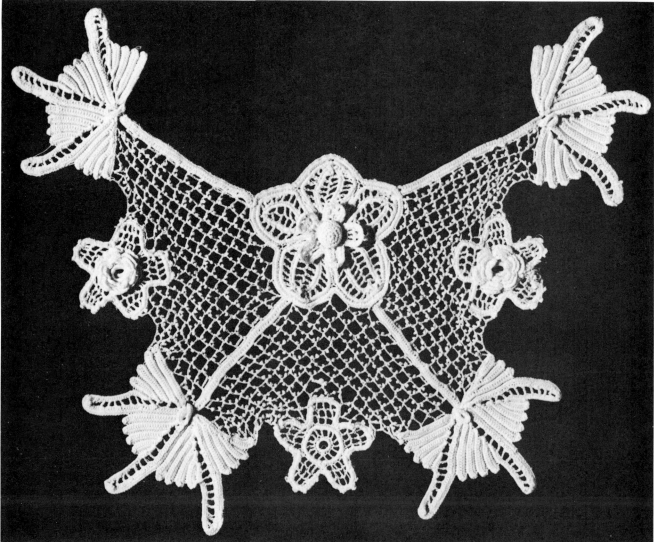

Filet Crochet

Filet crochet creates designs with open and solid squares. This type of crochet originally imitated net darning, which was called real filet. Filet crochet was very popular in America in the first part of the twentieth century. It was easy to do because it required only simple crochet stitches. It could be used for dainty handkerchief corners, lingerie, household linens or bedspreads, depending on the type of thread and size of hook used.

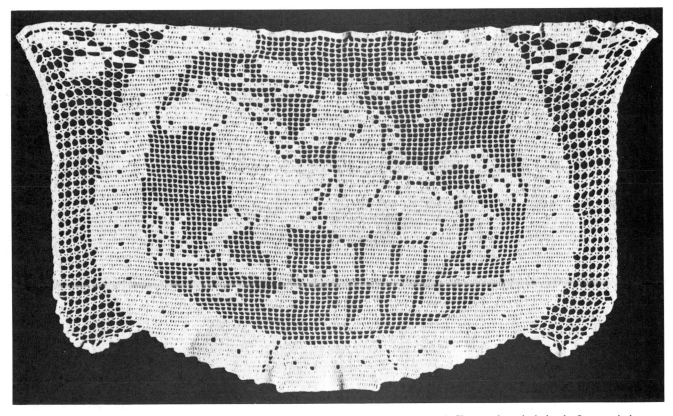

A filet crochet chair back. Lacet stitch was used in the side sections.

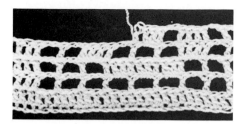

Above: Sample of filet crochet made with double crochet stitches and chain-2 spaces.

Below: Sample of lacet stitch mesh for filet crochet.

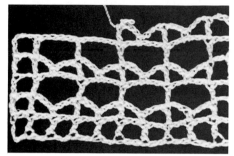

Construction

Filet crochet is usually made with double crochet and chain stitches. Open squares (called spaces) are made by working a chain-2 space between two double crochet stitches. Solid squares (called blocks) have double crochet stitches in place of the chains. Sometimes triple crochet and chain-3 spaces are used.

A fairly common variation of the background mesh of filet crochet is called "lacet stitch." Rows of small triangles alternate with rows of five-sided spaces. Regular spaces or blocks can be worked over the row that makes the five-sided spaces.

Patterns are worked out on squared paper.

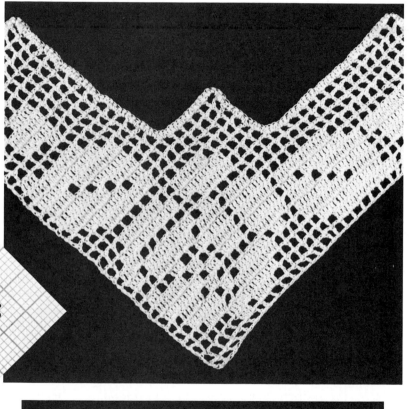

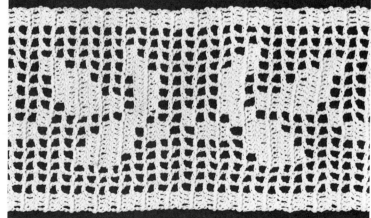

Above: Pattern on squared paper of a rose design corner motif.

Above right: Filet crochet corner motif with a rose design.

Right: Leaf design in a filet crochet insertion.

Special Crochet Stitches

An important clue to identifying crochet is that chains rather than single threads, twisted threads, or braids connect parts of the design. Several crochet stitches are exceptions to this rule because they have or appear to have single threads.

Knot Stitch

Knot stitch seems to result in single threads going from stitch to stitch, but actually the threads are in groups of three—the loop of a single crochet stitch is pulled long and a second single crochet stitch is worked between the loop and the single thread.

Crochet knot stitch looks a lot like netting, but netting has single thread loops and one knot per loop, while knot stitch has three-thread loops and appears to have several knots per loop.

Looped Crochet

The most common looped crochet stitch is usually called *loop stitch* or *fur stitch*. The thread is taken around one or two fingers or a gauge, such as a ruler or strip of cardboard, as the stitch is being made. Alternating rows of loop stitch and plain crochet make a textured trimming for hats, sweaters, and pillows, or the "fur" on toy animals. A single row of loop stitch makes a fringe. The loops of two strips can be joined with plain crochet, crochet insertion, or by "braiding" loops from one strip through corresponding loops of the second strip, as with hairpin lace (see page 27).

Another looped crochet stitch, sometimes called *river stitch* is made by holding the preceding row along the bottom of a gauge and bringing a loop of thread through that row and up to the top of the gauge where the stitch is completed. A single row of these confined loops makes an interesting contrast with plain crochet; a shawl or pillow cover could be made with successive rows. Loops can be spaced and grouped to make a variety of designs.

Loops can be incorporated in crochet by pulling up the thread in certain stitches extra long as in a shell pattern.

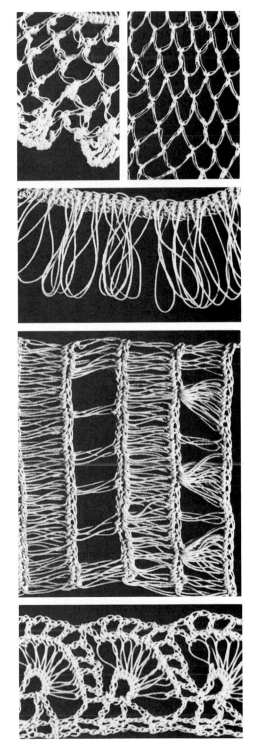

From top to bottom:

Handkerchief edgings of crocheted knot stitch.

Looped crochet, fur stitch.

Looped crochet, loops confined and spaced.

Crocheted edging incorporating loop stitch.

Wrapped Stitches

Two special crochet stitches that are occasionally seen in items made in the late 1800s and early 1900s are *roll stitch* and *Clones knot stitch.* Both involve wrapping the thread around the hook a number of times.

The *roll stitch* (also called *bullion stitch*) makes a column of wrapped threads. It is made by taking the thread around the hook a given number of times (five to twenty) before putting the hook into the next chain or stitch, then pulling the loop through all the turns of thread on the hook. There is a single thread going from the top of the roll to the base of the stitch on the back of the work.

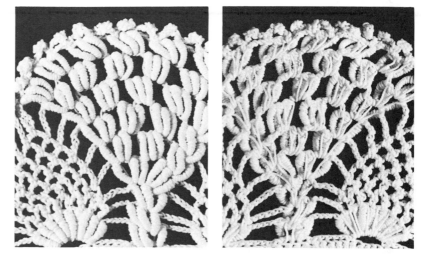

Below, left to right:

Making crocheted roll stitch.

Doily edging with a "pineapple" pattern and roll stitch.

Reverse side showing single threads at the backs of the roll stitches.

The *Clones knot* (named for the town of Clones, Ireland, near the border of Northern Ireland) makes a solid disk of wrapped threads. These were included in some of the larger and more complicated Irish crochet pieces as grapes or berries, to add texture to leaves or flowers, and as large picots in the background mesh, either singly or in threes or fours. A Clones knot is made by wrapping the thread alternately around the hook and around both the hook and the chain a number of times. The thread is then pulled through the loops on the hook, bringing the ends together in a circle with the chain inside.

Below, left to right:

Making a Clones knot.

Clones knots on crocheted snowflakes.

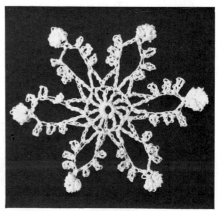

Hairpin Lace

Hairpin lace is a variation of crochet that developed in the latter part of the nineteenth century. It was not mentioned in an 1870 needlecrafts book, but it was included in the *Dictionary of Needlework* published in England in 1887, which said hairpin lace was "so called as the work is made between the prongs of an ordinary hairpin, though bone imitations of the same are used." By 1885 the "imitations" had become the general rule. "Weldon's Practical Crochet," an English newsletter, reported that "hair-pin or Krotchee crochet . . . derives its name from the fork or hair-pin

This shawl of fine lustrous wool features circular motifs and "braided" strips of hairpin lace combined with rows of small crocheted rings and loops of loose chain stitch.

like article upon which it is worked, which may be had in metal or bone, or even a coarse hair-pin can be employed." The work was called staple work if a bent wire like a large staple was used. It was also called fork crochet.

Narrow strips of hairpin lace resemble portions of some patterns of lace made in Malta. When these strips were basted to a pattern and the spaces filled with needle lace stitches, the resulting lace was called *Imitation Maltese Lace*. Eventually hairpin lace of any width was called *Maltese crochet*.

Needlework magazines from the early 1900s show hairpin lace used for collars, bonnets, parasol covers, and doilies and as edgings for handkerchiefs, aprons, nightgowns, camisoles, and household linens. In more recent years, hairpin lace has been used for afghans, shawls, pillows, and other articles made of yarn.

Construction

To make hairpin lace, strips of loops are worked around parallel rods. Various styles of hairpin lace looms are now available that permit the looped strip to be made any desired width, depending upon how far apart the rods are. The thread is wound around the rods by turning the loom. After each turn, a crochet hook is used to make a stitch through the top loop at the middle of the strip, forming a center rib. This rib is usually made with a single crochet stitch, but other stitches can be used to get different effects.

After a strip of loops is removed from the loom, it can be used to make an edging, insertion, or an individual motif, or strips can be joined to form wider articles such as afghans or shawls.

Strips can be joined to other strips by:

1. "Braiding" — alternately pulling a loop from one strip through a loop from the adjacent strip, making a "braided" effect. Working two or more loops together makes a heavier "braid."

2. Crocheting through the adjacent loops of two strips, or working crochet panels between two strips, using matching or contrasting thread.

The outer edge is usually finished with plain or fancy crochet, or the loops may be "braided" through each other. Sometimes the loops are left loose to form a fringe. The rib may be worked off-center to make longer loops on one side for fringe.

Loops are sometimes twisted before they are joined or as the edging is being made to create a different effect.

Curves and scallops are formed by grouping a number of

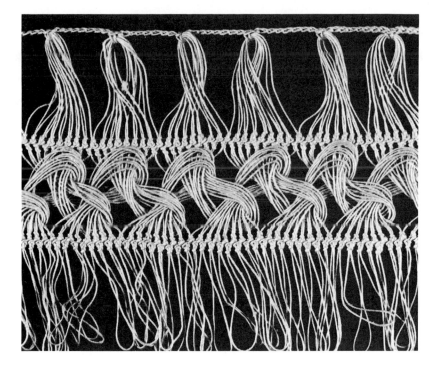

Hairpin lace edging made with two wide strips of loops "braided" together in groups. Loops along one edge are joined in groups with a crocheted chain and the loops along the other edge are loose, forming a fringe.

loops together with one crochet stitch. Occasionally tatting is used to connect strips or to finish outer edges.

Round or square motifs can be made with a crocheted center or by running a thread through the loops on one side of the strip and knotting the thread tightly to pull all the loops together at the center. The beginning and ending threads of the "rib" are tied together, and then the outer loops are connected with plain or fancy crochet. These motifs may resemble Tenerife lace, but the threads do not cross at the center, and the "rib" is distinctive.

The loops along one edge of a strip of hairpin lace were crocheted together in groups to form the center of this medallion.

● Distinctive Features

1. Strips of single thread loops with a crocheted rib in the center. The strips may be narrow or several inches wide.

2. Curves and scallops formed by grouping several loops.

3. Crocheted (or sometimes tatted) edgings and joinings.

Strips joined by "braiding." (See page 27.)

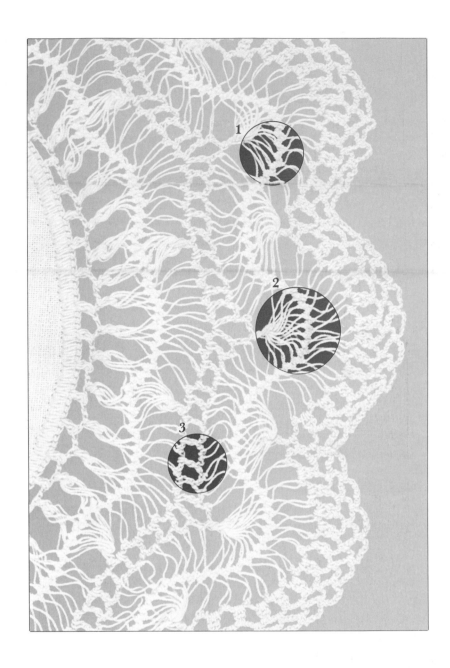

Hairpin lace edging on a doily, made with two strips of loops joined and edged with crochet.

A strip of chain stitch hairpin lace.

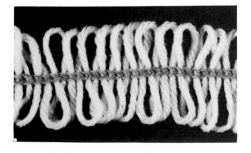

Chain Stitch Hairpin Lace

A simpler but less stable way to make strips of loops is called *chain stitch hairpin lace*. Yarn is wrapped around a hairpin lace loom or a gauge with an open center strip. After the desired number of loops has been wrapped, a chain stitch is crocheted along the center around each thread. This makes a narrow straight rib, rather than the wider, zigzag rib made with regular hairpin lace. The chain stitch rib can be made a different color than the loops, which cannot be done in regular hairpin lace. However, the chain stitch does not hold the loops firmly, so a snag will pull up adjacent loops. Strips of chain stitch hairpin lace can be joined using all the ways shown for hairpin lace and can be formed into round or square medallions.

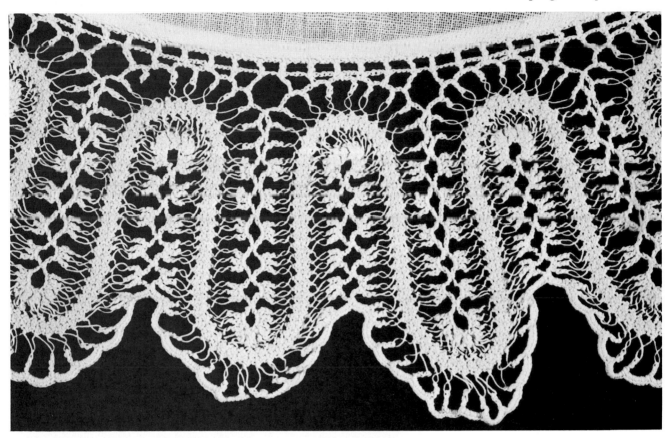

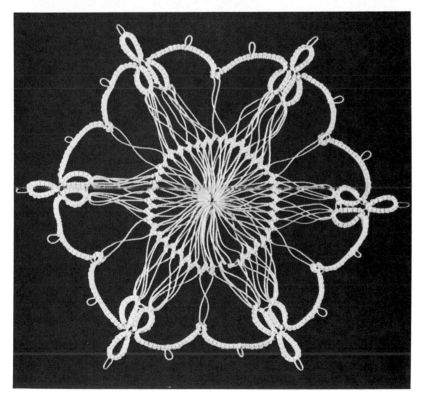

Above: Hairpin lace "serpentine" edging, made with one strip of loops curved back and forth, joined and edged with crochet.

Left: Snowflake medallion made by tying the loops on one side of a strip of hairpin lace together at the center and joining the outer loops singly and by threes with tatting.

Broomstick Lace

Broomstick lace, also called *jiffy lace*, is a variation of crochet that might be confused with hairpin lace because it also has single thread loops held in a twisted position with crochet stitches. However, broomstick lace does not have the center rib in the strips of loops that is characteristic of hairpin lace.

Broomstick lace was featured in American needlework magazines in the 1970s for sweaters, vests, afghans, shawls, and purses. A large knitting needle or piece of dowel (or a broomstick) and a crochet hook are the tools required.

Right: This broomstick lace capelet was made with four-ply yarn.

Below: Sample of straight broomstick lace worked in crochet thread to show the construction.

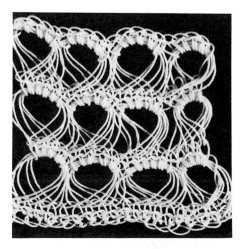

Construction

Broomstick lace starts with a chain or a row of crochet. The last loop is pulled up long enough to slip over the needle.

Loops are pulled up through each chain or stitch and placed on a large needle. These loops are worked off in groups, and as many single crochet stitches are worked along the top of the group as there are loops in the group. These two rows are repeated throughout the article, or they may be interspersed with rows of plain crochet. It is usually made with yarn, and variations depend on changes in the color and the type of yarn used.

Broomstick lace can also be formed into square or circular medallions by adding extra crochet stitches or chains.

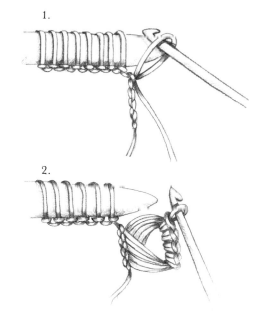

Making broomstick lace

1. With a crochet hook, long loops are pulled through each chain or stitch in the preceding row and placed on a large needle.

2. Groups of loops are worked off together, then single crochet stitches are made along the top of the group.

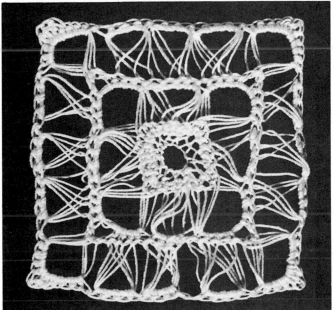

Broomstick lace medallions.

Knitting

Knitting, like crocheting, is a way of making a fabric with a continuous thread by pulling one loop of thread through another. The looped construction is more apparent in knitting than in crochet. In knitting, all the stitches are held as loops on two or more needles, rather than only one stitch being held on a hook as in crochet.

Although knitting is undoubtedly an ancient craft, some of the very old fabrics from archaeological diggings that were first identified as being knit were later found to be sprang (see page 62). The earliest pieces of actual knitting have been found in Syria and date back to the second or third centuries A.D.

Knitting produces a very elastic fabric that is especially well suited to making garments to cover the irregular shape of human hands, feet, and heads. Knitted sandal socks (with the big toe separate from the others to allow for a sandal thong) found in Egypt date from the fourth or fifth centuries A.D. These show sophisticated shaping, indicating that the art of knitting had been highly developed by that time. Knitting was probably brought to Spain from the Near East, following the Moorish conquests in the eighth century. Knitted silk gloves used at New College, Oxford, England, in 1386 are thought to have come from Spain. A fourteenth-century painting, *The Visit of the Angels,* by Bertran, about 1390, which was formerly part of the altar of Buxtehude Abbey, Germany, shows the Madonna knitting, picking up stitches around the neck of a garment. The needles and method are the same as used today.

In Britain, as in other northern countries, knitting first developed among shepherds as a way of making warm garments. In late medieval times, knitting gloves, caps, and stockings for sale was largely a masculine occupation. All family members helped knit articles for domestic use. Children were taught to knit as soon as they were old enough to hold the needles. In groups, they would chant traditional knitting songs in which the words and rhythm of each verse indicated the number of stitches to be increased or decreased. Men and women knitted as they rode or walked to market and when they gathered in sociable groups. A knitters guild was founded in France in 1527. Its patron saint was St. Fiacre, son of a Scottish king, which lends some credence to Scotland's claim that knitting was invented there.

In 1546 Henry VIII granted a license to two Florentine merchants to sell luxury goods in England for three years. Among the items he selected for himself was a pair of gloves knitted of silk. Queen Elizabeth was given a pair of knitted stockings in 1561. She greatly preferred them to the cloth hose she had been wearing, and her serving women soon learned to make them.

When Queen Elizabeth's forces defeated the Spanish Armada in 1588, one of the Spanish ships was wrecked on Fair Isle (between the Orkney Islands and the Shetland Islands north of Scotland). Some stories say the Spanish sailors taught the islanders how to knit. Other stories say the islanders knew how to knit and copied the colorful patterns in the clothes of the Spanish sailors. Those patterns formed the basis of the multicolored Fair Isle knitting that is still popular. On other British islands knitters also developed distinctive styles. The words *jersey* and *guernsey* (the names of the two largest islands in the English Channel) came to mean specific styles of sweaters. *Aran*, or *fisherman knits*, with cables, diamonds, and bobbles, developed on the Aran Isles off the west coast of Ireland.

An openwork pattern forms the cuffs of these knitted gloves.

Although knitting was primarily a utilitarian craft for producing warm garments, it was also used to make lacy fabrics. St. Bridget, who died in 1335, is credited with introducing lacemaking to Sweden. According to legend, at the age of twelve Bridget received help from an angel as she worked at knitted lace. In the Middle Ages Swedish nuns knit laces of gold and silk. In 1575 Mary Queen of Scots sent Queen Elizabeth headdresses, collars and cuffs, and nightcaps that she had knitted.

By the early 1700s patterned knitting in colored silk was a fashionable pastime for people of leisure. By 1760 fashion called for white stockings and gloves made of fine cotton thread. Heavy

A variety of knitting needles, including a set of five fine steel double-pointed needles in a wooden case, two pairs of single-pointed needles with knob ends, and a circular needle with a flexible connection between two pointed ends.

duties placed on foreign laces encouraged the use of knitted trimmings. Openwork patterns grew increasingly intricate, using finer thread and thinner needles, for collars and cuffs, mittens, fischus, bonnets, and doilies.

In Colonial America four-year-olds were taught to knit stockings and mittens. As they mastered these, they could advance to finer work. Young ladies knit silk stockings with openwork designs, often including initials, to wear with their wedding dresses.

Throughout Europe orphans were taught to make lace as a means of supporting themselves. This was usually bobbin lace, but in the 1760s prizes were given to workhouse children in Dublin, Ireland, for "thread lace made with knitting needles."

Delicate ring shawls have been knitted on the Shetland Isles since the beginning of the nineteenth century. The gossamer thin yarn is spun from the very fine wool that grows around the necks of the islands' sheep. The shawls are knitted on fine steel needles in traditional openwork patterns with names such as Horseshoe and Print of the Waves. The shawls are about six feet square, but weigh only about three ounces. The entire shawl can be drawn through a wedding ring.

The industrial revolution in Europe and America created a middle class with the leisure to do handwork for pleasure. Mills produced large quantities of fine threads, replacing the laborious hand spinning. As suitable thread became available, knitting, crochet, and other handwork became fashionable pastimes. *The Ladies' Knitting and Netting Book* was published anonymously in 1837 and was soon followed by other instruction books. They contained a few directions for articles of clothing, but the majority of patterns were for doilies and mats to satisfy the Victorian desire to have fancy covers on all household possessions.

The British Compulsory Education Act of 1870 included the provision that all girls must be taught knitting, including knitting socks on four needles.

Knitting is best known today as a technique for making sweaters, mittens, socks, and baby clothes. We usually do not think of knitting as a way to make lace, but many of the stitches produce a lacy texture. When knitting is done with fine thread and thin needles in an openwork pattern, the result is lace. Knitted lace is sometimes called Viennese lace.

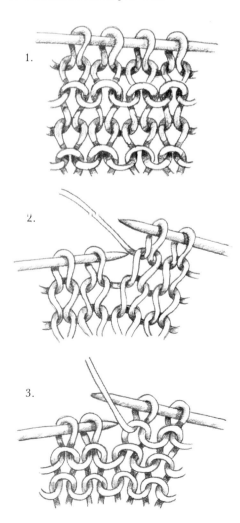

Round knitting on four double-pointed needles.

Construction

Stitches are held on two or more knitting needles, sized appropriatly for the thread being used. Knitting needles are usually made of metal or plastic and occasionally of wood. They range in size from a 1.0 mm to 12.7 mm in diameter or more. Two needles are used for straight knitting (back and forth). These needles usually have one end pointed and the other knobbed. These were formerly and more descriptively called knitting pins. Four or five double-pointed needles are used to knit circles or cylinders, working round and round. The number of needles used depends on the number of stitches, the design, or both. If the design is divisible by three (a six-sided snowflake, for example), it is convenient to use four needles (three holding the stitches and a working needle knitting the stitches off of one of those three needles), but if the design is divisible by four (an eight-pointed star, for example), it is easier to use five needles, so the pattern sequence will be the same on each of the holding needles. Circular needles, which have two short pointed ends and a flexible connection, can be used for larger circles or cylinders, or for straight knitting.

The working thread is looped through each stitch in turn, with the stitch being dropped off one needle as the loop forms a new stitch on another needle. If the stitch is dropped behind the new one, a smooth knit stitch is formed. If the stitch is dropped in front of the new one, a bump or purl is formed. (The back of a knit stitch is a purl stitch.) When working back and forth, if all rows are knitted, the fabric is ridged with alternate smooth and rough rows. This is called *garter stitch*. If the rows are worked alternately knit and purl, the fabric is smooth on one side, rough on the other—the characteristic texture of hosiery and sweaters. This is called *stockinette stitch*.

Open spaces in lace knitting are usually formed by wrapping the thread around the needle in one row and working that loop as a stitch in the next row. Larger holes are made by casting off a few stitches in one row and casting on the appropriate number of stitches in a subsequent row.

Two or more stitches are worked together to keep the number of stitches even or to change the direction of the stitches.

Knitting

1. Garter stitch, made by knitting every row, back and forth.
2. Stockinette stitch, made by knitting across and purling back, knit side.
3. Stockinette stitch, purl side.

● Distinctive Features

1. Areas of stockinette or garter stitch.

2. Holes separated by twisted threads.

3. Holes surrounded by garter or stockinette stitch.

Soft, elastic lace (unless it has been starched).

Stitches looped through each other.

Knitted doily with a design of elongated leaves in stockinette stitch, finished with a crocheted chain stitch mesh.

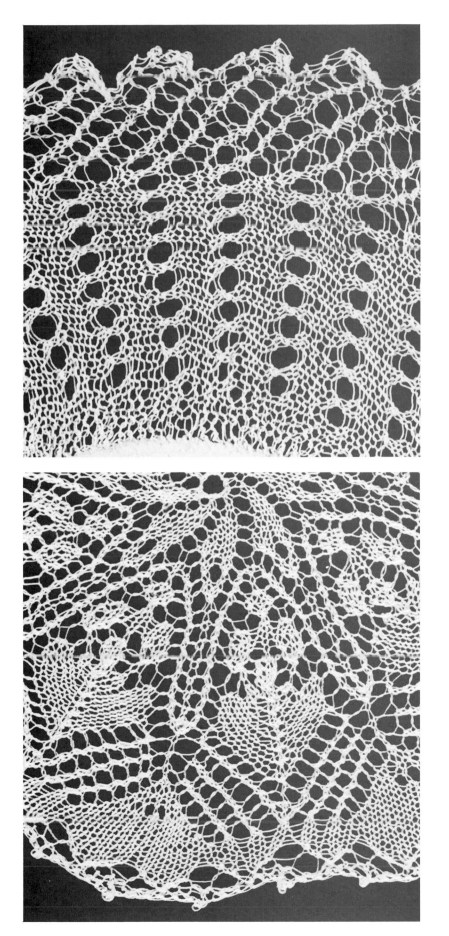

Left: Knitted edging on a doily, with rows of holes surrounded by garter stitch and a border of holes separated by twisted threads.

Below left: A round knitted doily with hearts around an eight-pointed star.

Below: Knitted edgings and an insertion.

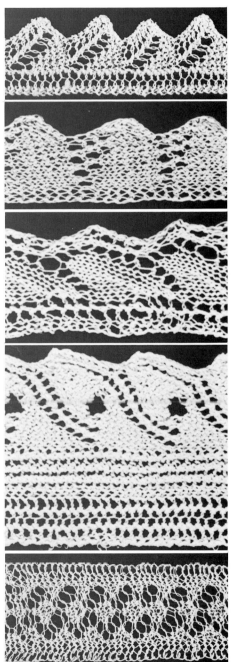

Knotting

Tying two or more threads together

By trial and error our early ancestors in all parts of the world learned to tie secure knots, using whatever fibers were available, to make snares and nets to capture fish and animals and to carry food and household goods. As food supplies became more dependable and civilizations advanced, people had the time to make utilitarian articles more decorative. Nets were made with finer fibers and smaller mesh, eventually resulting in netting that was used for clothing and household decoration. Designs were introduced into netting by weaving fibers into the mesh or by varying the size and spacing of the meshes.

In countries around the eastern end of the Mediterranean, a *knotted lace* developed. Knotted lace is similar to netting, but is worked with a sewing needle, while for netting, the thread is wound on a shuttle and the knots are tied around a gauge.

As weavers made fabrics on looms, they tied knots in the warp threads at the ends of the weaving to keep it from unraveling. These simple fringes developed into decorative knotting called *macrame*.

Tatting is another form of lace made with knots. The double stitch, which forms the rings and chains in tatting designs, is a double half hitch knot.

Knotting Techniques

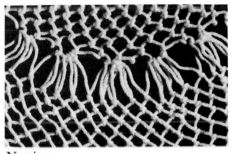

Netting

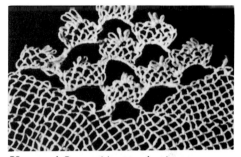

Knotted Lace (Armenian)

Macrame

Waffle Work

Tatting

39

Netting

People have been tying fibers together to make nets since before the dawn of history. Nets over 10,000 years old have been unearthed in Switzerland. Archaeologists have found evidence of net bags, hunting and fishing nets, and garments of net in all parts of the world. Few actual samples remain from prehistoric times, but pictures and carvings show how nets were used. Decorative nets appear in Egyptian art as early as 2130 B.C.

Because nets are so much stronger than their fragile appearance would suggest, they were important in many cultures not only for their usefulness and decorative value, but also in a magical sense. In myths and superstitions, nets were reputed to be able to pursue and devour, but they were also credited with the power to protect and cure.

Scandinavians in the eighteenth and nineteenth centuries hung festive netted roof panels in which evil was supposed to get entangled so it could not enter the house. Indians in Alaska hung nets over doors and windows for the same purpose. In northern India, women hung nets to repel evil spirits before childbirth. On the other hand, there are tales of evil forces using nets to capture their victims and becoming entangled in their own nets.

This small evening bag and gloves are netted.

Legends tell that netmaking was taught to humans by super-natural beings. For example, a Maori folktale from New Zealand tells that a war chief far from home saw a band of faeries catching fish without hooks or lines. As the faeries fled from the mortal, one was caught in their net when it snagged around a bush. The war chief seized her and her basket containing the tools for making nets. He took her to his village where she taught the Maoris the secrets of knotting the delicate looking but strong and useful nets.

The Greek poet Homer mentions the cauls and networks of gold worn by Trojan women. At about the same time the Prophet Isaiah (Isaiah 3:18 23) enumerated the articles of jewelry and clothing that the Lord would take away from the haughty daughters of Zion, including cauls (networks) and veils. Cauls of that period are defined in *Smith's Bible Dictionary* as headdresses made in checkerwork, long like a scarf, worn by women for ornament.

Two gauges, two netting shuttles, and a netting needle

Exquisite nets were made in medieval times in Europe. In the eleventh century the Spanish soldier-hero El Cid was reported to have presented a netted tunic to the Sultan of Persia.

Close-fitting netted caps are seen in pictures painted in the thirteenth and fourteenth centuries. By the middle of the fourteenth century, the excessive luxury of veils, worn even by serving girls, caused Edward III of England to issue an Act in 1363 forbidding the wearing of veils of silk or any other material that cost more than tenpence.

In the 1500s network embellished the costumes of the soldiers of the Spanish king Charles V, as well as the trappings for their horses.

Netting came to America with the colonists. Netting with large-scale mesh was used for hangings and canopies on four-poster beds. (These are popular today in colonial restorations.) Netting with smaller mesh was used to decorate smaller household articles and clothing. A letter about Martha Washington commented that netting was a source of amusement for her, and that the younger members of the family were proud to have their dresses trimmed with the netting she made.

Much of the netting made in the sixteenth to nineteenth centuries was used as the basis for net darning (filet). In the Victorian era, netting, in which the lacy patterns were formed by making mesh of different sizes and varying the groupings of the meshes, was popular for table covers, doilies, collars, cuffs and gloves, either as edgings or for making the entire article.

Construction

The thread is wound on a shuttle or netting needle.

A foundation loop of string is firmly attached to some object such as a door handle, heavy pin, cushion, or even a rock, so that tension can be applied as each knot is tied. The loops are knotted

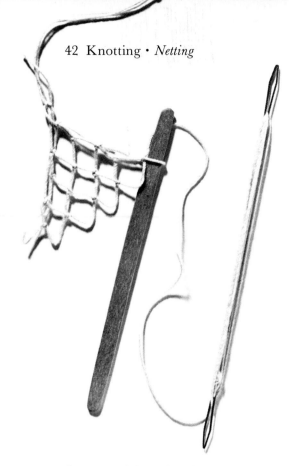

Square mesh is worked diagonally, beginning with one loop. A loop is added at the end of each row until the desired size is reached.

● Distinctive Features

1. Various sizes of mesh

2. Several mesh worked into one loop

3. One knot joining several loops

Single thread mesh with knots that do not slide along the loops

Netted doily started with mesh worked into a foundation loop that was pulled tight.

around a gauge (a flat stick or a rod), which keeps the mesh uniform.

The knot is a slipknot tied around a previously made loop, then pulled up so the loop is incorporated into the knot.

Netted strips are started with mesh tied over a foundation cord, or the first row of mesh can be made directly into fabric, using a needle. Circular mats are started by making a number of mesh in the foundation loop. This loop is then pulled up and tied tightly. The work continues round and round.

Netting patterns are made by varying the size of mesh by using gauges of different widths or by wrapping the thread more than once around the gauge, by making more than one mesh in a loop of the preceding row, or by bringing several loops of the preceding row together in one mesh.

Square mesh is made with all the loops the same size. A square is started at one corner and worked diagonally, increasing one loop at the end of each row until the desired number of mesh has been reached, then decreasing at the end of each row to the opposite corner. Square mesh is the basis of the very old type of lace called net darning or filet.

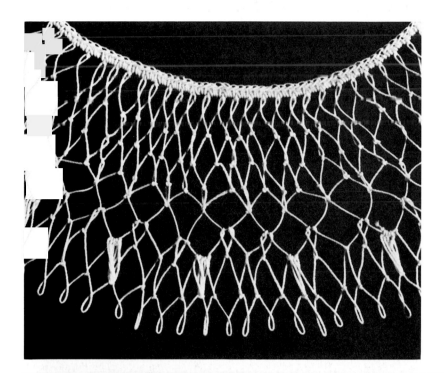

Left: Part of a netted collar. The design is made by spacing and grouping loops. The neck edge is crocheted.

Below: Netted edging worked into crocheted chain stitch loops around the linen center of a doily. The pattern includes two sizes of mesh, groups of loops tied together and groups worked into single loops. The design of squares was added by darning.

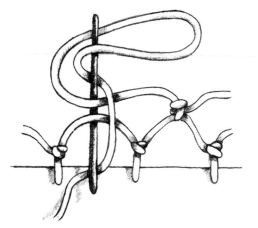

Knotted lace stitch.

Knotted lace edgings.

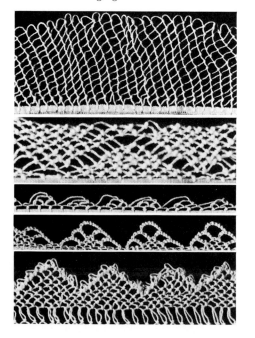

Knotted Lace

Knotted lace, which is worked with a sewing needle, originated in the countries at the eastern end of the Mediterranean. It is commonly called *Armenian lace*. Making this lace was considered to be a necessary accomplishment of every Armenian woman. Girls as young as three learned the skill. The lace was made to decorate garments and head coverings and to enrich household textiles.

Similar laces—for example, Turkish, Rodi (Rhodes), Smyrna, and Nazareth laces—were made in other eastern Mediterranean areas. Details of how the needle was placed and how the thread was twisted around it varied, but the results were essentially the same. Three-dimensional flowers and leaves, sometimes in brilliant colors, were made with this technique.

Construction

Only one knot is used, a knot similar to the knot used in netting. However, the knot simply goes around the supporting thread (as in tatting and the half hitches in macrame), while the knot used in netting locks the working thread to the supporting thread. No gauge is used to keep the mesh uniform—the uniformity depends on the skill of the lacemaker in keeping the loops the correct size.

Most designs are made by varying the size of the mesh, or by making more or fewer mesh in succeeding rows, as in netting. Tufts of extra loops (not caught in a subsequent row) are sometimes used to fill a mesh space to make filet-type designs.

Plain mesh is sometimes decorated with darned-in lines.

In general, the mesh of knotted lace is smaller than in netting, and the designs are more complicated.

A few rows of knotted lace stitches make a dainty edging for collars and handkerchiefs. Edgings can be worked directly on the fabric, on a woven tape, or on a crocheted chain.

● Distinctive Features

1   Single thread knotted mesh
    which looks like netting, but the
    loops are generally smaller and
    the designs more complicated

2. Various sizes of mesh

3. Designs made by grouping and
    spacing the loops

Knots that can be slid along the
loop

Knotted lace doily with several sizes of
mesh, grouped and spaced.

The round motifs in this knotted lace mat
were started with tatted rings of long
picots. The long grouped stitches are called
lovers' knots. The picot mesh has a small
loop beside each regular mesh.

Macrame

Knotting has been used to make decorative fringes since earliest times. Ancient sculptures from Babylonia and Assyria show decorative knotted fringes. Weavers knotted the warp threads at the ends of pieces of fabric to keep them from unraveling. Then to make the fringes more decorative, additional rows of knots were made and different knots were developed.

The word *macrame* comes from an Arabic word used by the

Macrame purses became popular when interest in this craft revived in the mid-1900s.

Italians to mean a towel or the material the towel was made of. The towels were usually finished with a knotted fringe so macrame came to mean a knotted fringe, and eventually the term was used for all forms of decorative knotting.

Working macrame with the unwoven threads of a fabric or separately with fine thread was an important lacemaking technique before 1500, especially in Italy and Spain, where it was used for church linens and vestments and other trimmings. Macrame was a well-developed art in the seventeenth and eighteenth centuries throughout Europe. In the mid-nineteenth century, macrame again became very popular. Decorating styles of the period favored elaborate trimmings such as knotted fringes and tassels. Macrame was used in making or decorating clerical vestments and table coverings, lampshades, umbrellas, baby carriages, purses, and accessories.

On sailing vessels the crew worked with knots and ropes. In their spare time, they knotted useful and decorative articles such as mast skirts, bunk pockets, mats, belts, and purses. The work was usually called *square knotting* or *fancy rope work*. The knotted articles were often used for barter when the ship was in port.

When fashions for home furnishings and clothing swung toward simplicity in the 1920s, ornate macrame did not fit in, and the craft passed into obscurity. In the 1960s interest in macrame revived. Plant hangers, wall hangings, belts, and purses knotted with heavy cord (often jute) became very popular.

We do not think of today's macrame as lace, but examine the patterns and imagine them made with fine thread.

Construction

Macrame requires no tools except fingers, but the work must be fastened to a firm support. It is worked with multiple threads, either with the unwoven threads at the end of a piece of fabric or with threads attached to a cord or rod, or into the hem or selvage of fabric, with *larks head* knots.

Some macrame is made entirely with *square knots*. The square knots are usually tied with two threads around two "filler" threads.

A series of square knots tied with the same threads makes a straight bar or *sinnet*. Making only one half of the square knot (a *half knot*) repeatedly with the same threads produces a twisted sinnet.

An attractive lacy pattern is made with alternating square knots: two threads from two adjacent square knots in the preceding row are used; the knot is tied with the threads that had been the filler threads.

Half hitches are tied over a "knot bearer," a thread held horizontally or diagonally. A row of half hitches makes a solid line horizontally or diagonally in the design.

Overhand knots are used in making knotted fringes, either by tying one thread around one or more adjacent threads or by tying

Macrame knots

1. Larks head knot.

2. Square knot.

3. Two half hitches, (left) as tied, and (right) pulled together.

4. Overhand knots, (left) one thread tied around the others, and (right) all threads tied together.

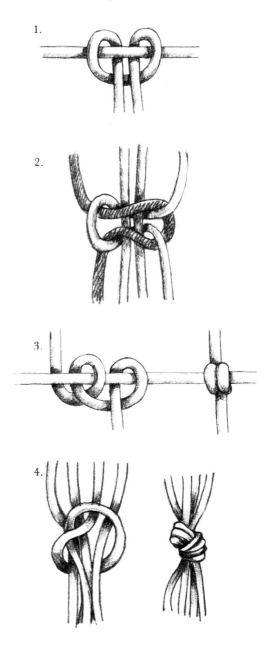

the knot with two or more threads held together.

The woven shawls called *redozos* made in Peru and Equador with Ikat weaving (the yarn tie-dyed for a specific design before weaving) have a wide border of knotwork and a fringe at each end. The knotwork is done with overhand knots. The background is rows of closely spaced alternating knots, and the design is outlined with open spaces formed by including more than two threads in a knot. The more elaborate the pattern in the knot-work—birds, flowers, coats-of-arms, or messages—the higher the status the shawl gives to the woman who wears it.

Distinctive Features

1. Square knot sinnets

2. Half knot twisted sinnets

3. Alternating square knots

4. Horizontal and diagonal bars of half hitches

5. Overhand knots

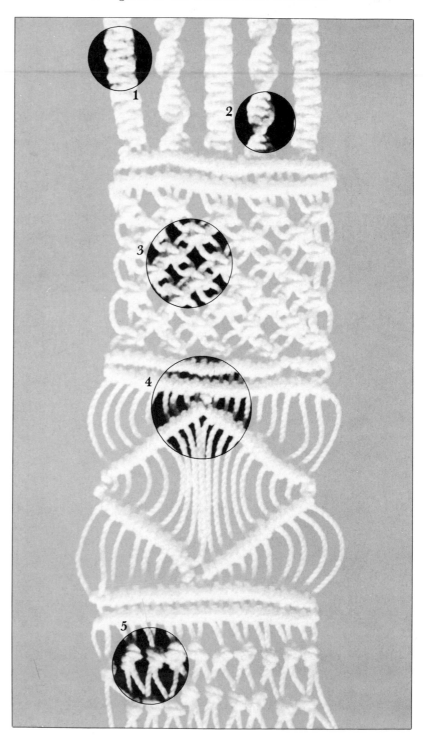

Sampler of macrame knots.

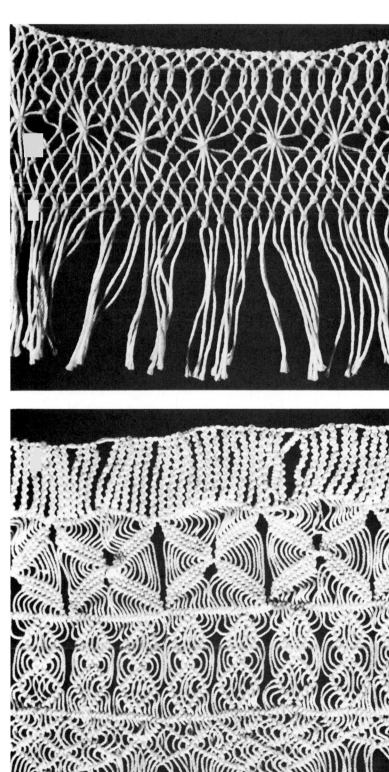

This macrame fringe, worked from a Finnish pattern, is made with overhand knots.

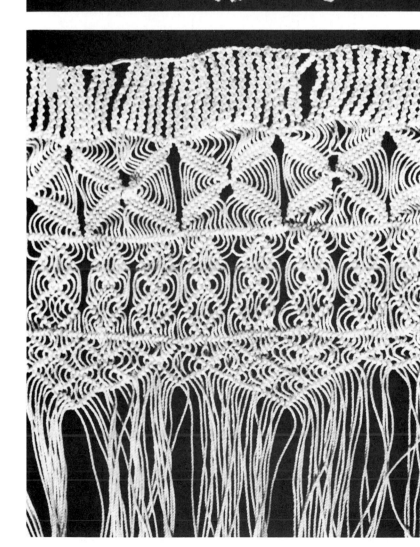

The design of this macrame fringe, probably made for a table or piano scarf, has twisted sinnets and horizontal and diagonal half hitch bars.

Waffle Work

The technique of making mats and other articles by wrapping several layers of thread across pegs or notches on a frame in two or three directions and then tying knots at all the points where the wrapped threads cross has been around for many years without acquiring a name that is generally known. The most descriptive name we have found for it is *waffle work* because the texture reminds one of a waffle. Some of the names that have been used include the word *weaving* (for example, Weaving Frame, Speed-O-Weave, Hexagonal Weaving, Lap Weaving), but the fabric is held together with knots rather than by interweaving the threads.

Graumonts and Weston include the technique in their *Square Knot Handicraft Guide*, which gives examples and directions for types of knot work that have been traditional crafts of seamen for hundreds of years. They called the technique *cross clove hitched work* and *pillow top work*, or *puff ball work* when wrapped threads in the top layer were cut between knots to make tufts.

Below right: A doll models a baby bonnet of waffle work.

Below: Waffle work is made on a small square frame.

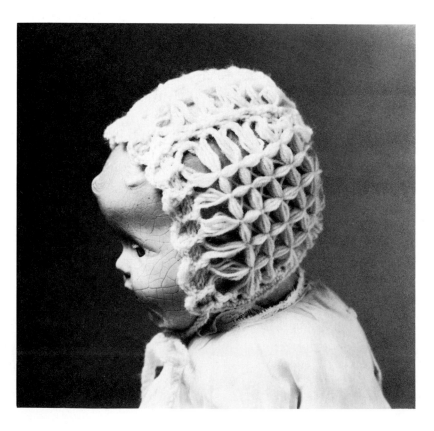

Other names that have been used for this technique are *frame work* and *mat work*. Needlework magazines in the early 1900s gave directions for "cross thread work" and "cross bar mats." Suggested uses were baby caps, sacques, fascinators, tidies, and hot dish mats and also large articles such as rugs and bedspreads.

Commercially made frames for waffle work became available in America in the early twentieth century—the wooden Priscilla Adjustable Weaving Frame in 1915 and the Bucilla "new, improved Adjustable 'Waffle Weave' frame" in 1934. The direction booklet with the Bucilla frame said that waffle weaving was something "entirely new and appealing," but then added that it really was a "revival of an old art particularly featured in Blind Institutions and Veteran's Hospitals due to its utter simplicity."

Currently metal and plastic frames are available for making square and oblong or hexagonal shapes, with directions and kits for articles ranging from scarves to Christmas decorations.

This technique, using many layers of wrapped threads, has often been used to make heavy place mats and hot dish mats. These are too thick to be considered lace, but the pattern does consist of open spaces, made by knotting the crossed threads tightly together. When only a few layers of thread are wrapped on the frame, the result is a more open fabric, which does look lacy. Interesting patterns are made by using different colors in wrapping the frame and tying the intersections, and by adding decorative needlework.

Construction

A rigid frame the size of the finished article, with notches or pegs approximately an inch apart, is needed. The thread is wrapped from the top left peg (or notch) to the one straight across, back around the beginning peg, down to the next one, across, and so on. When the bottom peg has been wrapped, the loom is turned so the pegs can be wrapped in another direction. Wrapping the loom first with a layer of threads of one color and then with another color makes a fabric that is a different color on each side. Interesting patterns can be made by wrapping alternate pegs with different colors, or two or three pegs with one color and one with another, and so on. The basic pattern made on hexagonal looms consists of triangles. Larger triangles, hexagons, flowers, and stars can be made by wrapping a contrasting color around certain pegs.

After the frame has been wrapped, the threads are tied at each intersection so that the tying thread makes a cross on the other side of the work. The crossed clove hitch knot is actually two (or three) half hitches or buttonhole stitches, worked diagonally across the intersecting wrapping threads. A large tapestry needle

Schematic diagrams showing the basic forms of waffle work, and how wrapping with contrasting colors makes patterns:

1. Square, horizontal/vertical wrap, diagonal ties

2. Square, horizontal/vertical wrap with two colors.

3. Hexagonal, three-directional wrap, two colors.

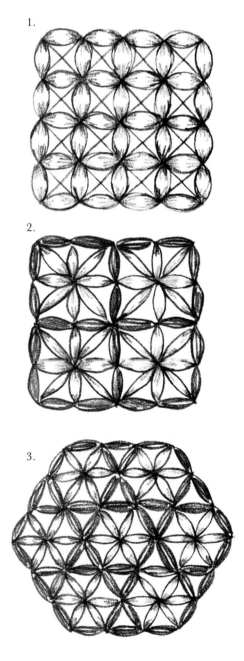

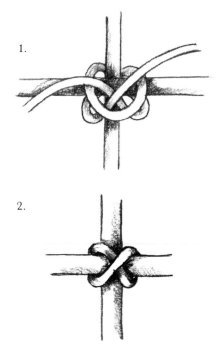

1.

2.

Crossed clove hitch knot

1. Front as worked, back of article.

2. Back as worked, front of article.

Waffle work doilies made with finer thread and additional needlework.

or a slender shuttle holds the tying thread, which may match or contrast with the wrapped threads. The tying thread may go from intersection to intersection along the wrapping threads or diagonally across the open spaces to produce a different texture.

If the top layer of wrapped threads is cut between the knots, little tufts or pompons are formed. The whole surface might be treated this way or only borders or designs.

Edges of waffle work articles are usually fringed by cutting the edge loops when they are taken off the frame. Sometimes the uncut loops are left loose or "chained" by pulling one loop through the next loop all around the outer edge.

Tatting

Tatting is lace made with rings and chains of double half hitch knots. Since it is a knotting technique, its roots go back into antiquity, but tatting did not develop into a popular way to make lace until after the middle of the nineteenth century.

Portraits from the eighteenth century show ladies holding what appear to be large tatting shuttles, but there is no tatted edging or doily to be seen—just a knotted thread. These knotted threads were used in a type of embroidery introduced into Europe from the Orient in the late 1600s. Knots were tied closely together on a thread, using a shuttle. The knotted thread was sewed onto fabric to give a textured effect, for example, closely spaced rows of knotted thread could depict the rough bark of a tree. Knotting was one of the few forms of handwork considered appropriate to work on in mixed company. Ladies could show off their shuttles of precious metal or carved ivory, and their graceful hand movements. They flirted with their shuttles as they did with fans and challenged the gentlemen to try to tie the knots.

Someone eventually learned how to tie a series of double half hitch knots in such a way that they could be pulled up to form a ring, and tatting was invented. In macrame, half hitches are tied over a knot bearer thread. In tatting they are started the same way, but then must be transferred so that they slide along the shuttle thread. This maneuver is so difficult and frustrating for many beginners to learn that one marvels that tatting was invented!

Both knotting and tatting were called *frivolité* in France, but that name seemed too frivolous for the English. The name *tatting* was first used in print in a little book called *The Ladies Handbook of Millinery, Dressmaking and Tatting*, published in 1843. In the preface the writer described tatting as being a very difficult kind of work, but said that it had been a favorite ornament for children's and other dresses, and that the instrument used in making it could be obtained at fancy needlework establishments. Only three simple examples were shown. The reason the name tatting was used is unknown, but it may have referred to the ragged, tattered appearance of strings of unconnected knotted rings. Not until the mid-1800s were techniques developed for joining tatted rings with picots as the rings were being made. It then became possible to make an actual fabric with a tatting shuttle, joining ring to ring and rows of rings to other rows, rather than just making individual rings that were later painstakingly sewed or tied together.

Other theories about the origin of the name *tatting* are that it came from the French word for *touch,* or the Italian word for *tight,* or from the *ta-ta-ta* sound made by some shuttles as the thread is pulled between their close-fitting ends.

In 1850 Mademoiselle Eleonore Riego de la Branchardière, the Englishwoman who popularized crochet in Britain, published the first of her eleven books on tatting. Before she published her first tatting book, she worked out a way to join tatted rings as they were being made. She used a netting needle instead of a shuttle so it could go through the picots. This was quicker than sewing or tying the rings together, but it did not hold the parts in a fixed position.

Drawnwork mesh, drawnwork and macrame, and tatting decorate bathroom towels.

In 1851 a better way to join tatted rings was described in a little booklet called *Tatting Made Easy, and how to join with the shuttle explained and exemplified.* The author only identified herself as "a Lady." Her method is still used today — a loop of the ring thread is pulled up through the picot so the shuttle can be slipped through the loop. Using this method, joinings are made easily and stay firmly in position. Riego described this joining method in her second tatting book and made no further mention of tatting with a netting needle.

The next major development in tatting was the chain — a curving bar of double half hitches connecting rings or even making up the entire design. In the early books on tatting, bars were made by using a threaded needle to work buttonhole stitches over the thread connecting the rings. Working double half hitches on a second thread, using two shuttles, was first described by Riego in 1864. The chain occurred in only one pattern and little attention was drawn to it, so other tatting designers did not immediately recognize its importance. This development, however, greatly expanded the design possibilities of tatting as well as speeding up the work.

Treasures in Needlework, by Warren and Pullan, published in England in 1870, gave instructions for tatting (which Pullan described as an art "among the best adapted for showing to advantage a pretty hand") and gave directions for three projects: an infant's cap crown, an edging, and a sleeve trimming. Tatted rings were connected with picots, but bars were made using a needle and making buttonhole stitches. The center of the cap crown

Tatted insertions and edgings trim a young girl's dress.

and spaces between tatted sprigs in the sleeve trimming were filled with needle lace stitches. This book was a compilation of articles that had been published in a British magazine, so the tatting instructions had probably been written several years before 1870, before the authors had become familiar with Riego's 1864 book. *Treasures in Needlework* contained directions for 170 projects in crochet; 106 in braiding, embroidery, etc.; 39 in netting; 32 in knitting; 18 in point lace; and only 3 in tatting. The distribution may reflect the preference of the authors more than the general popularity of the various forms of handwork.

Caulfeild and Saward's *Dictionary of Needlework*, published in 1882, included a long section on tatting. Chains were made with shuttles. As in Pullan's earlier directions, the first half of the double half hitch was called the *English stitch* and the second half the *French stitch*.

A Frenchwoman, Thérèse de Dillmont, published the first edition of her comprehensive book on needlework in 1886. Known in English as the *D.M.C. Encyclopedia of Needlework*, it has been translated into many languages and reprinted in many editions. It was selected as one of the forty French publications "most useful in women's education" at the Chicago Exhibition of 1893. It includes a chapter on tatting, elaborating on structures already known, and includes working with several colors.

Needlework books and magazines published in the early part of the twentieth century showed tatting combined with crochet and also with Tenerife lace, rickrack, medallion tape, and coronation cord. Tatted medallions were appliquéd to fine machine-made net to make collars, yokes, jabots, and similar accessories. Tatted medallions were inserted into fabric to give the effect of cutwork embroidery.

In America the popularity of tatting waned during the 1930s, revived in the forties, almost disappeared during the sixties, and then revived again in the late 1970s.

Tatting seems to be the only lacemaking technique known by the people who are currently making up crossword puzzles. A three-letter word meaning "make lace" (tat) is included in many puzzles.

Construction

Thread is wound on a tatting shuttle. These are made in many shapes and sizes. The most common ones are of metal or plastic, but they are also made of wood, ivory, bone, horn, and mother-of-pearl. Some shuttles have removable bobbins on which to wind the thread. If the shuttle does not have a point or a hook at one end, a crochet hook or a pin is needed to make the joinings. The double stitch, which is the basis of tatting, is a double half hitch knot.

Tatting designs are made up of rings of *double stitches*, connected by single threads or by *chains*, which are curving bars of double stitches. Loops of thread, called *picots*, are characteristic of

Tatting stitches

1. Double stitch.

2. Picots are loops of thread between stitches.

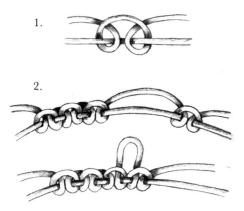

1.

2.

tatting patterns. They are used to make the designs lacier and to join rings and chains.

To make rings, the shuttle thread is wound around the fingers of one hand, forming a ring. The shuttle, which is held in the other hand, goes around the ring thread to form the half hitch knots (the double stitches). These must be transferred so the shuttle thread that made the half hitch becomes the knot bearer on which the half hitches slide. This transfer is accomplished by releasing the tension on the ring thread as the shuttle thread is pulled taut.

Rings are made using only the shuttle thread. Chains are made using a second thread (generally called the ball thread) secured across the fingers instead of wrapping the shuttle thread around the fingers as in making a ring.

Joinings are made by pulling the ring (or ball) thread through a picot so the shuttle thread can be slipped through the loop.

In the 1800s crochet tatting, using a straight-shafted crochet hook, and needle tatting, using a long thin needle with an eye, were described in needlework publications. In both methods, the double half hitches are made on the hook or needle and the support thread is then pulled through them, avoiding the tricky transfer step in regular tatting. These methods have recently been revived; tatting needles and Japanese tatting hooks are available from lace supply outlets.

Tatted netting, made by joining small rings to the threads between rings of the preceding row, is used as edgings, veils, and as part of larger tatting patterns.

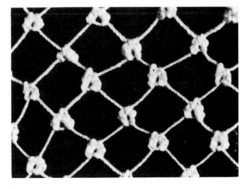

Tatted netting.

● Distinctive Features

1. Rings of double stitches

2. Picots, short

3. Picots, long

4. Rings (or chains) connected with picots

5. Single threads between rings

6. Chains of double stitches between rings

Above left: A strip of tatted medallions made with rings. The center is a ring of long picots. A double row of rings completes each medallion, with a small ring joined to a picot of the center ring, alternating with larger rings joined to each other.

Left: Popular cloverleaf tatted edging made with rings and chains.

Right: A thistle in free-form tatting.

Below right: Tatted doily made with five rows of different ring and chain patterns.

Below: Tatted edgings made with rings.

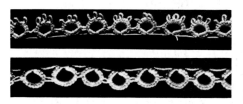

Different weights of thread and number of picots vary the same basic pattern.

Double row of rings alternating up and down—the third joined to the first, the fourth to the second, and so forth.

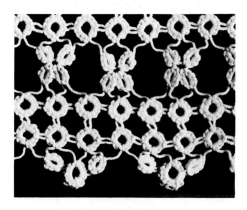

This wider edging has three double rows of rings, alternating up and down, joined in different patterns.

Left: Mat combining tatting and crochet (contemporary, made in the Orient). The small rings and narrow loops are tatted; the wider loops and large circles are crocheted.

Below left: Tatting variations: twisted node stitch (each half of the double stitch repeated several times), heart rings (forming a small ring within a larger ring by joining to a picot within the ring), and Cluny tatting (woven leaves formed by winding the ball thread back and forth from thumb to fingers and weaving the shuttle over and under these threads).

Below: An insertion and two edgings made with rings and chains. The picots along the straight side of the narrow edging are connected with a crocheted chain.

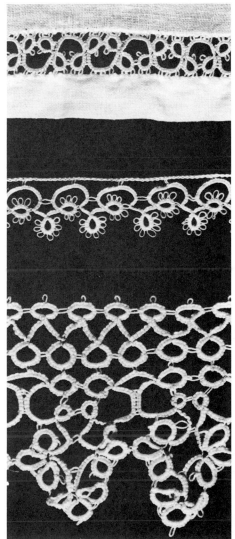

Crossing

Passing threads over and under one another

After our ancient ancestors learned that longer, stronger threads could be made by twisting fibers together, they learned that stronger cords could be made by twisting two or more threads together. Then someone playing with three threads crossed the right hand thread over the middle one, then the left one over the middle, and so on, and braiding was invented. Braiding with many strands made wider strips useful for belts and straps.

Braiders found that the crossings that made the braids were repeated in the lower part of the threads. Most braiders just considered this a nuisance that had to be untangled, but some realized that if both ends of the threads were held, the "extra" crosses could be "captured." Working in the middle of the strands, the braider could push the crosses both up and down. When they met in the middle they were secured in some manner. This "frame braiding" developed in many parts of the world and was used to make an openwork fabric. The technique is now called *sprang*.

Nearly all primitive cultures developed *weaving*. By intention or accident, weavers learned to manipulate threads during weaving to form openwork patterns—a form of lace.

Some cultures developed elaborate designs based on *interlacing* threads. Plain braids were made more decorative by manipulating the threads to create open spaces. The same techniques, done with finer threads wound on bobbins to keep them from tangling, developed into *bobbin lace*, with the stitches held by pins on a pattern fastened to a firm pillow.

Crossing Techniques

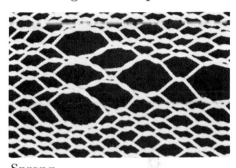

Sprang

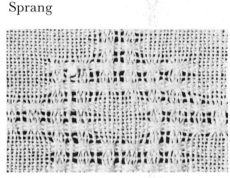

Weaving

Interlacing

Bobbin Lace

61

Sprang

Sprang is an ancient technique for making a textile, but you are not likely to find any among the old pieces of lace in your trunks and attics. You will see it in import stores, as lampshades from southeast Asia and as hammocks and shopping bags from Mexico and South America, and in the work of some of today's textile artists. Sprang is a technique that evidently developed independently in primitive cultures in many parts of the world, then dropped almost completely out of sight as people mastered the arts of knitting and weaving.

Sprang is the Scandinavian name for the technique of making a textile by twisting threads stretched between two horizontal bars. A more descriptive name is *frame braiding*. It is also called *knotless netting* and *Egyptian plaitwork*. Some of our ancient ancestors, twisting and braiding a few strands of fiber together, noticed that the twists repeated themselves at the other end of the strands. Building on this observation, they figured out how to make a fabric by attaching many threads to a frame and then twisting adjacent threads around each other. The twists, worked in the center of the frame, were moved toward the top and the bottom, eventually meeting at the center.

One hundred years ago, textile experts could not identify the twisted thread technique used to make a cap found at a burial site in Denmark, dating from around 1400 B.C. At about the same time, caps and bags made by a twisted thread technique were found in Egyptian graves dating from A.D. 400 to 700. One expert studying the Danish cap noticed that two small faults occurred symmetrically on either side of a center line, and she was able to figure out the method of construction. An Austrian expert studying textiles in the Ukraine found women in a small village making caps using a twisted thread technique that matched the Egyptian "mummy lace" and the Danish cap. Excavations in Peru have revealed sprang fabrics made with a high degree of sophistication, dated around 500 to 300 B.C. The ancient technique survived into modern times in areas of northern and eastern Europe, Spain, northern Africa, central Asia, and Central and South America.

Reexamination of ancient fabrics in museums disclosed that many pieces classified as knitted were actually sprang.

It is surprising that the textile experts a hundred years ago were not acquainted with the sprang technique because from about 1700 until 1850 military officers and city officials wore ceremonial sashes of silk sprang. George Washington's uniform, with a red sprang sash, is on display at the Smithsonian Institution in Washington, D.C. The sashes were about thirty inches wide when spread out and up to twelve feet long.

While making sprang, a rod, or "safety line," must be kept in the work to keep the twists from undoing themselves. It is very possible that Penelope's Web (the symbol of wifely faithfulness) was sprang rather than weaving. Pictures on Greek vases from Homer's time show frames of a type that could be used for sprang. In the *Odyssey*, written about 700 B.C., Homer tells that when Ulysses failed to return from Troy, many men sought to marry his wife, Penelope. She set up a great web on her loom and asked her suitors to wait until she had finished making a shroud for her father-in-law. By day she worked at the great web, but every night she undid the work. After three years, the men caught her undoing the work, and she had to complete it, although she devised other ways to deter the suitors until Ulysses returned. It would have been far easier for her to undo sprang every night than to "unweave" a woven fabric.

Textile artists today are using sprang by itself and in combinations with other techniques in small and large constructions, experimenting to achieve different textures and effects. A weaver might work a section of sprang with the warp threads on a regular

The openwork patterns at the top and bottom of this sprang lampshade (imported from the Far East) are actually mirror images but look different because an extra wire ring was placed in the lower section. Openwork weaving joins the two sprang sections.

loom, between two sections of weaving. Sprang might be combined with macrame and braiding in a wall hanging. Because sprang is a very relaxed, stretchy fabric, it is sometimes used as side strips in garments made of heavy handwoven fabric to provide comfortable ease in the garments.

Construction

Warp threads are wound around rods held in a frame. The rods are movable to allow for the change in length of threads as they are twisted. The threads in front are held in the left hand. The right hand picks up a back thread and drops off a front thread. The odd-numbered rows are started by bringing two back threads at the right edge forward; the other rows start by bringing one back thread forward. This has the effect of twisting each thread with the neighboring thread on one side in one row and twisting it with the thread on the other side in the next row, forming a twisted mesh.

Sprang may be interlaced firmly, but it is usually a very "relaxed" structure with an open, lacelike appearance when held out horizontally. No weft is used. A horizontal thread may be used at the center to hold the twists, or the threads may be "chained" at the center. The two ends are mirror images.

Designs are formed with holes. A hole is made by bringing one thread from the back and dropping off two front threads at one side of the hole and then bringing two back threads forward and dropping off one front thread. Holes can also be made by twisting each pair of threads more than once. Other patterns can be made by manipulating the threads in other ways.

A piece of sprang as worked will have a center line and the two ends will be mirror images. However, an object, such as a hammock or a shopping bag, made of sprang may not show the center line because the frame can be set up with long enough warp so that two objects can be made at one time and cut apart at the center of the warp.

The characteristic twist pattern of regular sprang can be duplicated using a threaded needle or a shuttle, such as is used in netting. A loosely crocheted chain forms the first row. Then the thread is taken through each loop in turn, with the needle or shuttle going down through the loops from right to left, and up through the loops on the return trip. Hammocks made with this technique at Twin Oaks commune in Virginia are described by Denison Andrews in *How to Make Your Own Hammock and Lie In It*. He also describes how to make a sprang hammock.

Sprang is worked with the threads wrapped between two dowels tied to a frame. The twists are worked in the center of the threads and are pushed to the top and bottom with rods.

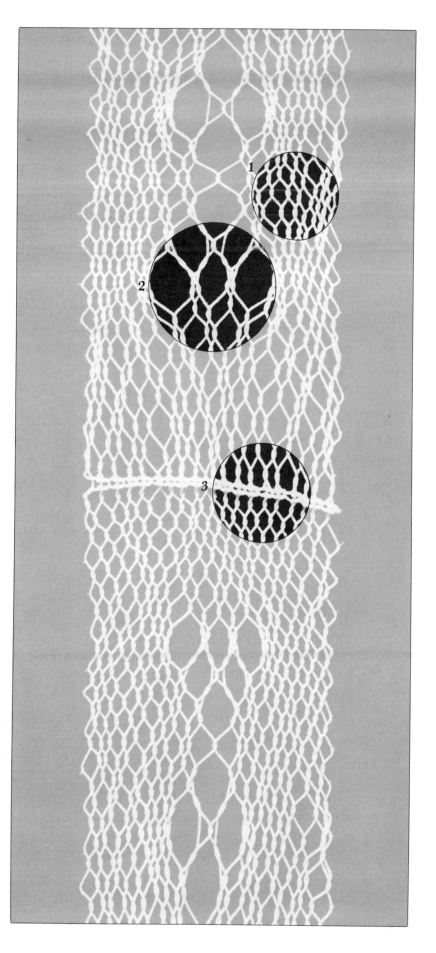

Sampler of basic sprang.

● Distinctive Features

1. Mesh formed of twisted threads

2. Designs of holes formed by twisting two or more threads together

3. Center line (this one is "chained")

Ends are mirror images (but the fabric may be stretched differently)

Weaving patterns

1. Leno weaves: single (1/1) and double (2/2).

2. Mexican lace weave.

3. Spanish lace weave.

4. Brook's bouquet weave.

5. Weft threads crossing over and under different numbers of threads.

6. Slits woven into the fabric.

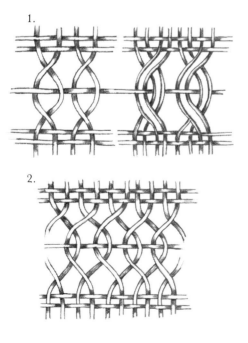

Weaving

Weaving developed in nearly all primitive cultures worldwide. Reeds woven in two directions produced serviceable mats. The same process was tried with grasses, roots, strips of bark, and twisted wool fibers. Looms were later invented to hold the lengthwise elements and to simplify the alternate raising and lowering of those elements as the crosswise elements were placed. Primitive looms and the materials woven by different cultures varied greatly, but the structure of the fabrics is basically the same.

Unusually well preserved woven fabrics have been found at several sites in Peru. Some date from around 1100 B.C. Agave fiber, cotton, and llama, alpaca, and vicuna wool were used. Surviving pottery, sculpture, and paintings show that the Indians of Mexico and Central America were also adept at weaving, but no actual pieces of fabric have been found.

The Pueblo Indians in what is now southwestern United States developed the art of weaving cotton to a fairly advanced degree by A.D. 700. They also wove fibers from the yucca plant, feathers, and strips of rabbit skin. Weaving eventually declined among the Pueblos, but the techniques were passed on to the neighboring Navajos, who used them with wool after the Spaniards introduced sheep in the seventeenth century.

Construction

Hand weaving is usually not considered to be a lacemaking technique, but some weaves do produce decorative openwork fabric. Openwork patterns are made by manipulating threads with the fingers, a hook, or a stick so the threads depart from their usual horizontal and vertical alignment. The most common lace weaves are leno and Mexican lace, Spanish lace, and Brook's bouquet.

Leno weave: Warp threads are crossed before the weft thread is put through. The simplest form is the 1/1, or single cross, in which two adjacent warp threads are crossed. A double, or 2/2 leno, has two threads crossed with the next two.

Mexican lace weave is a variation of leno in which the first thread crosses the second and the fourth threads, the third crosses the fourth and the sixth threads, and so on.

There are many variations of these crosses.

Spanish lace weave: The weaver works back and forth across small groups of warp threads, which are drawn together enough to leave spaces between the groups. The weft in this section is often heavier thread than in the rest of the weaving, or of contrasting color or texture. Various patterns are made by changing the number of warp threads in the groups, or the number of times the weft goes back and forth, and by interspersing areas of plain weaving.

Brook's bouquet weave: The weft is wrapped tightly around groups of warp threads (making a "back stitch"), pulling the warps together to leave open spaces.

Lacy patterns can also be woven by taking the weft threads over and under different numbers of warp threads.

Another way to make decorative open spaces in woven fabric is with slits. The warp is divided into sections, which are woven separately and then combined and redivided, according to pattern.

Lace weaving produces openwork designs similar to some types of drawnwork embroidery. In weaving, there is usually a plain selvage along the design area. Threads have not been cut and removed, so there are no raw ends secured by overcasting or buttonhole stitches.

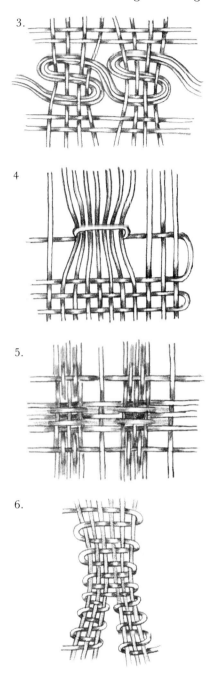

3.

4.

5.

6.

Woven mat with openwork pattern made by taking weft threads over and under different numbers of threads.

Interlacing

The simplest form of interlacing is braiding, or plaiting. Braids are made with three or more threads, crossed over and under, back and forth. In their simplest form, braids are like woven tapes, but with the threads running diagonally. Because the threads run across on the bias, braids can be shaped into ornate curves. Braids have been sewn to garments, curtains, and so on for decoration as straight borders and in fancy designs since prehistoric times. Using different weights, kinds, and colors of threads introduces pattern into the braids themselves.

Braided trims are called *passements*, from the French word meaning braid. Made with silk and metallic threads, they were used to trim the costumes of European aristocracy during the Middle Ages and into the Renaissance. Passements include braids, fringes, and trimmings ornamented with metal threads and beads. In the fifteenth century the term included laces, but as laces became more distinct and delicate in the sixteenth century, the French used the word *dentelle* as a general term for the lacier trims. The English word *lace* came into use at the end of the seventeenth century.

The designs of these snowflakes were adapted from Celtic interlacements and Chinese knots.

Taking some threads only partway across a wide braid, crossing and recrossing narrow braids in a pattern, or adding picots (loops) at the edges produce braids with openwork patterns. These could be called lace—there is no clear point of differentiation—but in general, braids are stiffer and plainer than lace.

Interlaced designs, developed from braids and knots, have been important in cultures all over the world. They often carry the symbolic meaning of eternity, continuity, and interrelatedness.

Chinese Knots

Elaborate knots and interlacements of silk cords have held an important place in Chinese folk art for thousands of years. In addition to adding design and color to robes, sashes, necklaces, lanterns, musical instruments, and temple decorations, specific knots carry symbolic meanings. Some express wishes for joy, good fortune, and long life, while others embody religious ideals.

The knot that Americans call the *double carrick bend, Solomon's knot,* or *true love knot* is known to the Chinese as the double coin knot. It represents two antique coins, overlapped, and connotes prosperity and longevity.

The *pan chang*, or mystic, knot has no occidental counterpart. This woven square, which forms the basis for many Chinese interlacements, is more complicated than it looks. It has two distinct layers; the woven back and front connect only at the edges. It represents one of the basic precepts of Chinese Buddhism—the cyclical nature of all existence.

The butterfly knot symbolizes the essential oneness of all being, a basic tenet of Taoist philosophy. It consists of a pan chang knot with double coin knots tied in two of the corner loops.

The *ju i* knot is three cloverleaf knots brought together with a fourth cloverleaf. Ju i means "everything according to your heart's desire." The knot is a symbol of great good fortune.

Button knots are used with looped knots to make fasteners for dresses, robes, jackets, and purses and vary in complexity from simple to highly complicated. These "frogs" are often used on western clothing to give an exotic oriental touch.

Celtic Interlacements

Metalwork with elaborate interlaced designs made by the Celts has been found in Switzerland, dating from around 2500 B.C. The Celts and their art spread from central Europe to the British Isles and Asia Minor.

Celtic artists in Ireland and Scotland from the eighth to tenth centuries brought the art of interlaced designs to a degree of perfection and intricacy that has not been equaled. Delicate designs illuminated manuscripts of the Gospels, such as the Book

Braid patterns

1. Nine strand braid
2. Opening in a braid formed by taking some threads only partway across.
3. An openwork pattern made by crossing four-strand braids.
4. Picots made by twisting two outer threads of a braid to make loops at the edges.

1.

2.

3.

4.

of Lindisfarne (before A.D. 698, at Holy Island off the east coast of northern England) and the Book of Kells (about A.D. 800, probably at Iona, off the west coast of Scotland). In these manuscripts, braids and knotwork patterns were combined with plant forms and animals, including birds, snakes, "doglike creatures," and humans. Legs, tails, necks, and tongues were extended to whatever lengths the artist needed to form the interlacements, which were more important to the artist than an accurate representation of the subjects.

Many of the interlacements in the borders, capital letters, and illustrations in the manuscripts can only be followed by studying the designs with a magnifying glass, although magnifying glasses had not been invented when these masterpieces were made. Fine interlaced designs were also represented in metalwork, and similar designs on a larger scale were carved into wood and stone.

Leonardo da Vinci, Albrecht Dürer, and Michelangelo (whose lifetimes spanned the period from 1452 to 1564) drew designs of Celtic knotwork and interlacements, which were printed for the use of painters, goldsmiths, weavers, and needleworkers. Interlaced bands of embroidery or braid were popular in costumes of men and women in the sixteenth century.

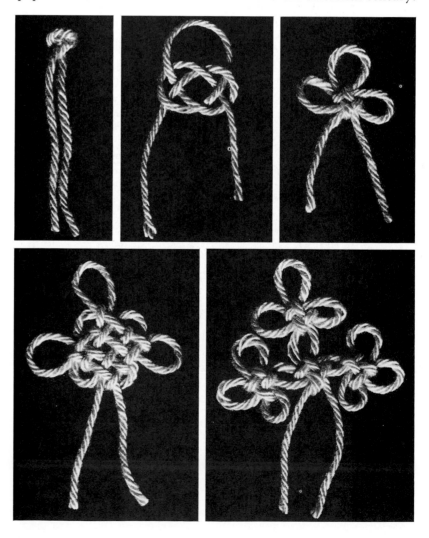

Left to right:

Chinese button knot.

The knot known in America as the double carrick bend, Solomon's knot, or true love knot is called the double coin knot by the Chinese.

Chinese cloverleaf knot.

Left to right:

The double-layered pan chang knot is the basis of complicated Chinese interlacements.

Four cloverleaf knots form the Chinese ju i knot, symbol of great good fortune.

A portrait of King Henry VIII (by the School of Holbein the Younger) in the Walker Gallery, Liverpool, England, shows interlaced designs in braidwork and embroidery on the king's costume and on the curtains beside him.

This Chinese butterfly knot is a pan chang knot with double coin knots tied in two of the corner loops.

A Celtic interlaced cross.

Celtic interlacements form an allover design on the curtain behind Henry VIII in a painting by the School of Holbein the Younger.

Bobbin Lace

Bobbin lace combines elements of sprang, braiding, weaving, and macrame. It probably developed, like macrame, from experiments in finishing off the unwoven warp threads at the ends of pieces of cloth. Threads were wound on bobbins to keep them from tangling, and new interlacing patterns were devised. The bobbins store the threads and make them easy to manipulate, and the weight of the bobbins pulls the stitches into position.

Bobbin lace is worked on a pillow, so it is often called *pillow lace*. Pins hold the stitches on a pattern, which is fastened to a firm pillow. Various styles of pillows are used, ranging from large flat pillows to cylindrical bolsters in a variety of sizes. When long lengths of an edging or insertion are being made, a bolster pillow is convenient because the work can proceed continuously. The pattern is fastened around the bolster. As the work proceeds, the bolster is turned, and the pins are taken out of the completed lace and moved forward as stitches are made. For making squares or circles of lace, or for making motifs such as flowers or leaves, a flat pillow is better because the work must be turned in all directions.

Both Italy and Belgium claim to be the birthplace of bobbin lace. The first definite references to it date from the end of the

Bobbin lace is made on a French-style pillow, with a collection of bobbins from eleven countries.

1400s. It was soon being made in many parts of Europe and became the main economic support of many areas as a cottage industry. Bobbin lace was almost as highly prized as needle lace. Different styles of bobbin lace were produced in different parts of Europe and were generally named for the place where they were made.

Bobbin lace was called *bone lace* in England. Until brass pins became available at a reasonable price in the latter part of the sixteenth century, fish bones or splintered chicken bones were often used as pins. Bone bobbins were also used. Small bones like the long slender bones from sheep's feet were used as is; larger bones were cut to shape. Sometimes bobbins were made from the bone of a roast served at a special occasion, with the bobbins inscribed to commemorate the occasion. In *Twelfth Night,* written in 1600, Shakespeare mentions "maids that weave their threads with bone," indicating that making bone lace was sufficiently widespread for his audiences to understand what was meant.

Beds-Maltese bobbin lace collar.

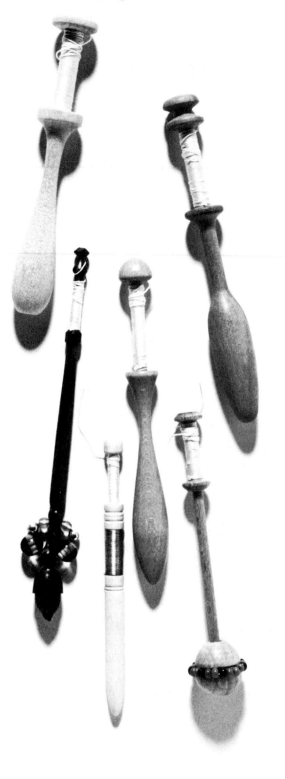

Different styles of lace bobbins.

Construction

Although complicated pieces of bobbin lace may require hundreds of bobbins, only four bobbins are used in each stitch, and only two movements are made with the bobbins—the *twist* (right bobbin over left with each pair) and the *cross* (left inside bobbin over the right—the bobbins change partners). The pattern made depends on the sequence of the twists and crosses and the order in which different pairs of bobbins are used.

When two pairs of bobbins are crossed, twisted, and crossed (CTC), the threads weave through each other. CTC with one pair working back and forth through each of the other pairs in turn produces "cloth" or "linen" stitch. This looks like ordinary weaving, except that two threads change direction at the selvage because the bobbins are worked in pairs.

Adding a twist (CTCT) "opens up" the weaving. Adding more twists makes the work more open. The "weaver" pair is usually given extra twists at the end of each row.

If CTCT, which is called *whole stitch,* is worked with each two pairs of bobbins across a row, and in the following row the CTCT is worked with one pair from each adjacent group in the preceding row, the stitches form a diagonal pattern.

CTCT repeated with the same two pairs of bobbins makes a braid.

Half stitch is made with just CT. One bobbin works back and forth with the crosses while the twists put the other threads in diagonal lines.

Spiders are often included in bobbin lace patterns. They are usually made with four or six pairs of bobbins. The upper legs of the spider are formed by twisting each pair of bobbins enough times to reach from the surrounding lace to the body, which is worked in cloth stitch (CTC). The bobbin pairs are again twisted to form the other legs as the threads go back into position to work the next stitches.

Many bobbin lace patterns include woven *leaves*, which look exactly like the raised leaves in net darning (see page 85) and some types of embroidery, but are made by weaving one bobbin over and under the threads of three other bobbins with TCT. Leaves are also called *wheatears, barley corns, tallies, fats,* and *leads.*

Leaves with pointed ends begin and end with a cloth stitch that brings the threads together.

Squares or *spots* are made like leaves, but without bringing the threads together at the ends.

Sections of bobbin lace are joined by a technique called *sewing,* although no needle is used. The thread from one of the working pair of bobbins is pulled up through the edge of the adjacent finished section of lace with a small crochet hook. The other bobbin of that pair is slipped through the loop, and both threads are pulled up to secure the joining.

Bobbin lace is sometimes combined with needle lace,

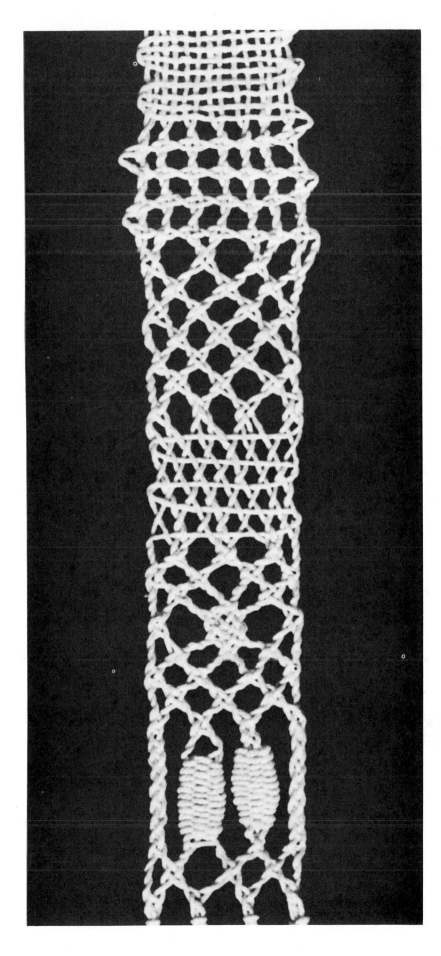

The stitches used in bobbin lace, *from top to bottom:*

Bobbin lace cloth stitch, made with one pair of bobbins weaving back and forth through the other pairs.

Adding a twist between cloth stitches makes a more open effect called "whole" stitch. Adding more twists makes the work more open.

Whole stitch worked diagonally, using one pair of bobbins from each of two adjacent groups in the preceding row, is a common background in Torchon bobbin lace.

"Half stitch" (made with CT) makes a light, delicate-looking filling.

In this spider, four pairs of bobbins are twisted to form the legs and woven through each other to make the body.

Squares (left) and leaves (right) are made by weaving one bobbin over and under the threads of three bobbins (with TCT). Leaves begin and end with the two pairs of bobbins together; in squares, the pairs are apart.

Braids (show on both edges) are made by repeating CTCT.

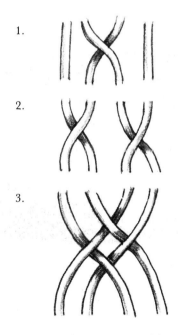

Basic bobbin movements used in making bobbin lace

1. the cross (C),
2. the twist (T),
3. CTC makes a "cloth stitch."

enhanced with needlework, or appliqued on handmade or machine-made net.

Dozens of types of bobbin lace are described in lace identification books. We will consider here only the major classifications of bobbin lace, with a few of the types you are most likely to find in your trunks and attics.

Bobbin laces all fit in two major classifications: *straight* and *free*. The design areas and the backgrounds of a straight lace are worked at the same time, usually with the same number of bobbins throughout. For a free lace, motifs are made separately and then joined. Bobbins are added as the design area of a motif widens, and then the threads are tied off and cut as they are no longer needed. The motifs are joined with bars or a net background worked either with bobbins or a needle, or they may be appliqued to net.

Distinctive Features

1. Cloth stitch

2. Half stitch

3. Leaves

4. Twisted threads

5. Braids

6. Whole stitch

7. Spiders

8. Fans

Above right: Torchon lace edging.

Right: Bobbin lace edging, Cluny type.

Straight Bobbin Lace

The following are common types of straight bobbin lace:

Torchon: Torchon lace has simple geometric designs made with a relatively small number of bobbins. There is a wide variety of patterns, which usually include spiders, scalloped fans, leaves, and diagonal whole stitch (which is sometimes called *Torchon net*). The word *Torchon* means "duster" or "rag" in French, and was given to this type of lace because it was simpler to make and cheaper to produce, compared with the much more elaborate laces favored by the aristocracy.

Cluny: Cluny lace also has simple geometric patterns. They often include rosettes of long slender leaves arranged like the spokes of a wheel, and diamond blocks of half stitch. Bars are braided rather than twisted. Cluny lace resembles sixteenth-century Genoese laces in the Musée de Cluny in Paris, from which it gets its name. Machine-made laces resembling Torchon and Cluny are currently being called Cluny.

Maltese: Maltese lace, often called *Beds-Maltese* because it was made at Bedfordshire, England, is like Cluny, but it is made with black or cream-colored silk thread. The designs are basically geometric, with short leaves forming crosses. The patterns include the eight-pointed Maltese Cross in cloth stitch.

Tape lace: The design in tape lace is formed with a curving strip, sometimes of varying width and including more than one stitch, worked continuously. The work in progress is joined to previously worked sections with "sewings." In the folk laces of Russia and eastern Europe, the strip is a straight tape shaped only at the U-bends; red and blue threads are often incorporated into the tapes. Only a few bobbins are needed even if the piece of lace is wide because only the width of the curving strip is being worked.

Tape lace is sometimes called *Russian lace*. It did not originate in Russia, but much of the lace made in Russia is of this type.

Torchon lace medallion with spiders and fans.

A Cluny lace edging with rosettes of slender leaves, chevrons of cloth stitch, diamonds of half stitch, and curves of whole stitch edged with braided loops.

Above: Beds-Maltese lace mat with eight-pointed Maltese crosses in cloth stitch, and broad leaves. The center square and the edging were made separately, then stitched together.

Right: Sample of tape lace worked with six pairs of bobbins. The tape curves to follow the pattern and is joined to previously worked sections.

Free Bobbin Lace

Honiton is the best known of the "free" bobbin laces. It was made in the town of Honiton in southwestern England. Flowers, leaves, scrolls, and indefinite shapes called *slugs* and *snails* are made separately, using fine thread, then connected by "sewing" pairs of bobbins into the small holes bordering a motif, working a braid or other filling across to an adjacent motif, "sewing" to it, and so on. Honiton motifs are also connected with needle lace stitches or appliquéd to net. Queen Victoria's coronation gown (1838), wedding veil (1840), and the christening gown worn by her children were trimmed with Honiton appliquéd on net.

Belgium Duchesse lace is a free lace similar to the English Honiton lace. Individual motifs are made separately and then connected with bobbin-made braids. Small flowers such as forget-me-nots, larger flowers such as primroses, and ribbed leaves are typical. Insets of *point de gaze* (a needle lace) are often included in Duchesse lace (see page 114).

Above: A Honiton lace sprig with flowers and leaves.

Left: Duchesse lace with typical small and large flowers and ribbed leaves, connected with braids.

Below: Dainty Honiton motifs with a variety of filling stitches were appliquéd as the border on a veil.

Needlework

Making stitches with a threaded needle

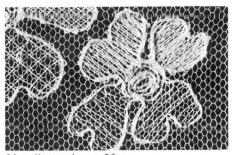

Needlework on Net

Embroidery has been used to decorate nets and fabrics from the time netmakers and weavers first became proficient at their crafts. Bands and simple designs could be worked into net without any tools. Embroidery was added to cloth and leather even before needles with eyes were invented—a sharp splinter of wood or bone would be used to make a hole through which a fiber could be pushed. As sewing techniques improved, ways were found to make openwork designs. These embroideries gradually developed into needle lace made of "stitches in air" supported on outline threads rather than on fabric.

Machines that could make fine netting were invented in the early 1800s. These nets were embroidered and appliquéd to make types of lace that had not been practical to make when fine netting had to be handmade with needle or bobbins.

Needlework is used to make a wide variety of decorative openwork fabrics.

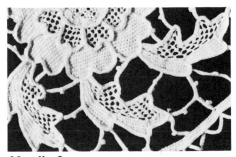

Needlework on Woven Fabric

Needle Lace

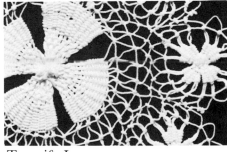

Tenerife Lace

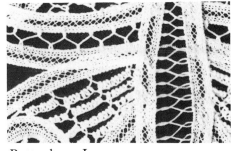

Battenberg Lace

81

Needlework on Net
Net Darning

Decorating square net by weaving bands of fibers through the mesh or by filling in squares to make a pattern is a lacemaking technique that has been used since prehistoric times. Ornamenting net with embroidery worked in various materials and stitches may have been introduced to Europe by returning Crusaders in the eleventh and twelfth centuries. By the thirteenth century, decorated net work was used for large articles, such as bedcovers and curtains, as well as for clothing. A cushion covered with decorated net work in St. Paul's Cathedral in London dates to 1295.

Decorated net work became a fine art in Italy, France, Germany, and England. It was widely used for ecclesiastical decoration. Religious symbols and pictures were darned into net and used for vestments, altarcloths, curtains, and wall hangings. Sometimes the whole article was made of net, but often squares of net darning would be alternated with squares of plain or embroidered linen fabric. Making these net squares was a popular needlework among the aristocracy in the sixteenth century. Catherine de Medici (1519–1589), queen of Henri II of France,

Net darning on a large scale was used to make this bedspread and pillow shams, which were lined and trimmed with light green fabric.

her two daughters, and her daughter-in-law Mary Queen of Scots spent hours darning designs on netting made by their ladies-in-waiting. An inventory of Catherine de Medici's property included hundreds of squares of "lacis." Mary Queen of Scots included her "ouvrages masches" in a will written in 1560.

Net darning came to America with the colonists. It was very popular in Europe and America during the Victorian era. Medallions and edgings darned on small-mesh netting continued to be popular in the early 1900s, and many of these laces were imported from the Orient. By the mid-1900s, net darning had almost disappeared as a pastime needlecraft in this country, but tablecloths and table mats continued to be made for sale by lacemakers in Germany, Mexico, and the Orient. With the availability of woven netting, net darning experienced a revival as a popular needlecraft in the 1980s.

As would be expected with any craft as old as net darning, it has been known by many names. In English-speaking countries, it has been known as filet, filet lace, real filet (to distinguish it from filet crochet), filet darning, spider work, and also by the French names *lacis* and *guipure d'art*. Modano is an Italian name for net darning that has extra threads run in to outline parts of the design and to form scroll-like details. This work was also called *Tuscan filet*. The name *antique filet* was used for net darning with woven leaf overlays and lace stitch fillings, which made parts of the design lighter in texture. Some authorities use the name *filet* for designs darned into hand-knotted net, and *net darning* when machine-made (woven) net is used.

Net darning forms the solid and the openwork design areas of this tablecloth.

Net darning stitches

1. Darning stitch goes over and under the threads of the net. It is used as a filling stitch and also to outline areas and to make stems, tendrils, and other lines.

2. Cloth stitch

3. Lace stitch

4. Raised woven leaves

5. Small and large laid stars

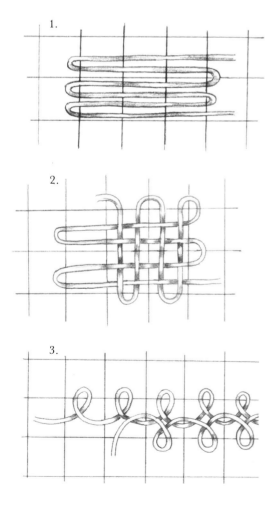

Before machine-made net became readily available, the first step in making net darning was to make a square or rectangle of netting. An undated article (probably from the 1890s), reprinted in the April-May 1977 *Olde Time Needlework* magazine, described the process as "not difficult to do, only a little tedious in the making," (which, of course, is why royal ladies had their ladies-in-waiting make the net). By the beginning of the twentieth century, machine-made nets were available. A 1905 article reprinted in the April-May 1979 *Olde Time Needlework* magazine said: "Many of the machine nets closely resemble the beautiful netting of olden days, which was so artistic and attractive, but was the result of weeks of patient work with the netting needles and mesh. It is seldom seen now, being a kind of 'lost art' to this hustling generation of fancy-workers." Sometimes designs were darned into crocheted mesh. Drawnwork embroidery was also used to make a net for darning.

Designs used in net darning are widely varied: geometric patterns, conventionalized flowers, animals, biblical scenes, mythological subjects such as cupids and dragons, monograms, coats of arms, and messages.

Construction

Hand-knotted net (see Netting, page 42) must be mounted in a frame to hold the net taut. Some of the machine-made net currently available is stiff enough so that it does not need to be mounted in a frame.

Net can also be made on a wooden frame that has nails or slots at appropriate intervals. The frame is made the size of the finished article. Threads are wound back and forth around the nails or slots. Cross threads are then knotted to the stretched threads to form the net squares, using a needle or shuttle. Decorative stitching is then worked on the net while it is still in the frame. This method is used by Mexican Indians who are noted for their net darning.

Stitches used in net darning:

Simple *darning stitch* (the filling thread weaving back and forth across the squares, over and under the net threads) and *cloth stitch* (the filling thread weaving back and forth, over and under the net and filling threads up and down and across the squares) are the most commonly used stitches.

Areas of cloth and darning stitch (and sometimes other stitches) are often emphasized by running two threads, or one heavier thread, around the outline with a darning stitch. These threads may also form stems, tendrils, leaves, etc.

Lace stitch: Buttonhole stitches are looped loosely over the top thread of a horizontal row of squares. On the return row, buttonhole stitches are made over the bottom thread of the same square, with the needle going under the vertical mesh threads and over the working thread of the first row.

Lace stitch can also be made by working the loops around the intersections of the net threads rather than looping over the threads of the net. This stitch makes a checkerboard effect of open and filled squares. It can also be worked diagonally. Lace stitches are sometimes worked with a finer thread to emphasize the laciness.

Raised woven leaves: Two or more threads are attached side by side across squares or over darned areas. These threads are then needle-woven (back and forth, in and out) without catching the background. Woven leaves are also found in some types of bobbin lace, but these are made with two pairs of bobbins rather than with a threaded needle.

Laid stars: Laid stars are usually worked over four meshes to make a four-point star or over sixteen meshes to make an eight-point star. Starting in the center, the thread is laid across the squares horizontally and vertically (and also diagonally for the large star) and caught under the net at the opposite edges or corners. The thread is then woven around the center of the star, over and under the laid loops.

Heavy (usually very soft) threads by themselves may form stars, flowers, leaves, and geometric patterns and borders.

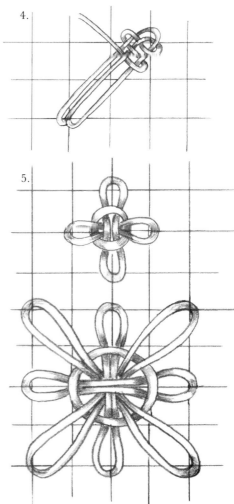

4.

5.

● Distinctive Features

1. Cloth stitch

2. Outlines of darning stitch (also stems, tendrils, etc.)

3. Raised woven leaves

4. Laid stars

5. Lace stitch

Small mat of net darning. This size of mesh (five to the inch) is commonly used for larger pieces such as place mats and tablecloths.

Right: Medallion of net darning. Imported, handmade medallions, edgings, and insertions were sold in American needlework stores in the late 1800s and early 1900s.

Below right: Diamond of net darning. Mythological creatures were popular themes for designs.

Below: Edgings of net darning. The designs in the top two are all cloth stitch. The third one has curved lines of darning stitch for stems. The bottom one has raised woven leaves. The net in the top three edgings has about twelve mesh per inch; the bottom edging has nine mesh to the inch. The shaped edges are finished with buttonhole stitch.

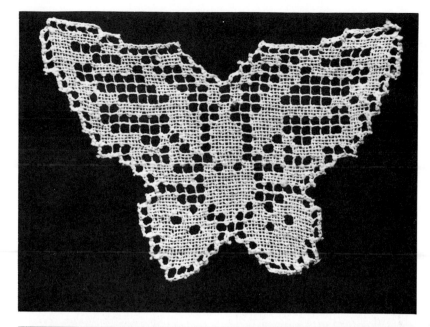

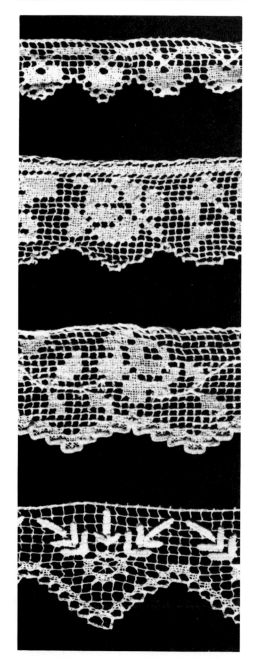

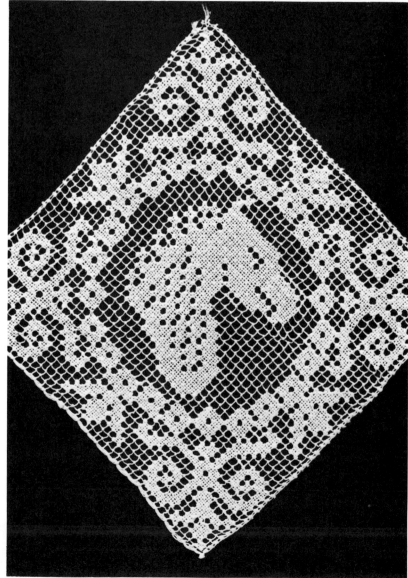

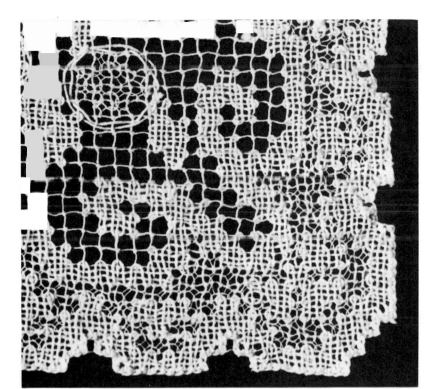

Left: Place mat of net darning. The design is mostly cloth stitch, accented with lace stitch and darning stitch outlining some areas.

Below: Doily made on hexagonal machine-made net, darned with heavy yellow and white thread. The edging is buttonhole stitch.

Needlework on Fine Net

Late in the eighteenth century, machines that had been developed for knitting stockings were adapted to make a lace mesh, but when the mesh was cut or a thread broke, the mesh unraveled. In 1808 John Heathcoat in Nottingham, England, invented a machine that made a strong net similar to the net made with bobbins. This enabled laces to be made much more quickly and therefore less expensively. Bobbin lace and needle lace motifs were mounted on the net background. Lacemakers could undertake much larger pieces of work since they did not have to spend their time making the background. The lace was made in wider flounces and whole garments rather than as trim.

The machine-made nets became the basis for new types of lace—needle-run, appliqué, and tambour. These laces were very popular during the Victorian era for dresses, flounces, and scarves. They were important parts of the Irish national lace industry, which developed during the potato famines in the mid-1800s.

Baby bonnet of needle-run lace. Very fine thread was used for the filling stitches and heavier thread for the leaves.

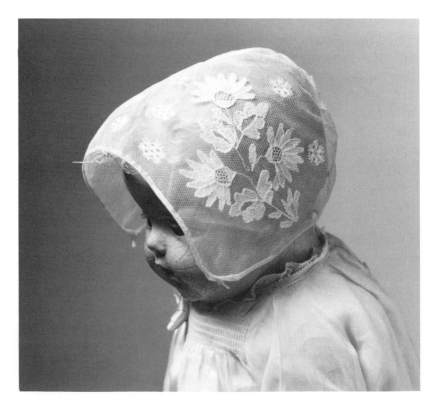

Flower spray of needle-run lace.

Needle-run

Needle-run laces are made by embroidering the net. Flower petals and other designs are outlined with stitches running in and out of the meshes, and may be filled with a variety of stitches using finer threads.

Appliqué

Dainty laces are made by appliquéing pieces of thin fabric to a mesh background. Organdy or fine muslin is laid over the net. The design is outlined with a heavy thread firmly oversewn to the fabric and the net with a fine thread. The background fabric is then cut away. The net may also be cut away from some areas—the center of a flower, for example—and the area filled with needle lace stitches. Stems and small leaves are often added with needle-run embroidery.

Carrickmacross appliquéd lace, named for Carrickmacross, Ireland, where it was first made, typically has "pops" (circles formed by working buttonhole stitches around one hexagon of the net) scattered through the design and an edging of "loops" (picots formed with the heavy outlining thread). Parts of the design are enhanced with needle-run stitches, and both the net and appliquéd fabric are cut away in some areas. Lace stitches may be added as fillings in these cutout areas.

Carrickmacross guipure does not have a net background. The design is outlined with thread and the background is cut away. The design pieces are connected with stitched bars.

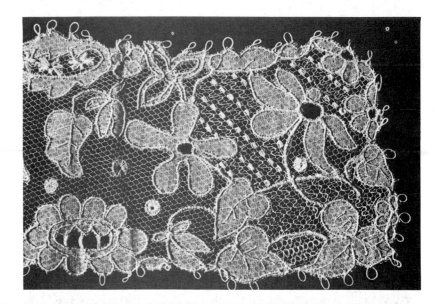

Right: Carrickmacross lace collar, with fabric appliquéd to fine net and the buttonhole stitch "pops," needle-run fillings, open areas, and looped edges characteristic of this type of lace.

Below: This Carrickmacross mat from Ireland combines appliqué and needlework on fine net.

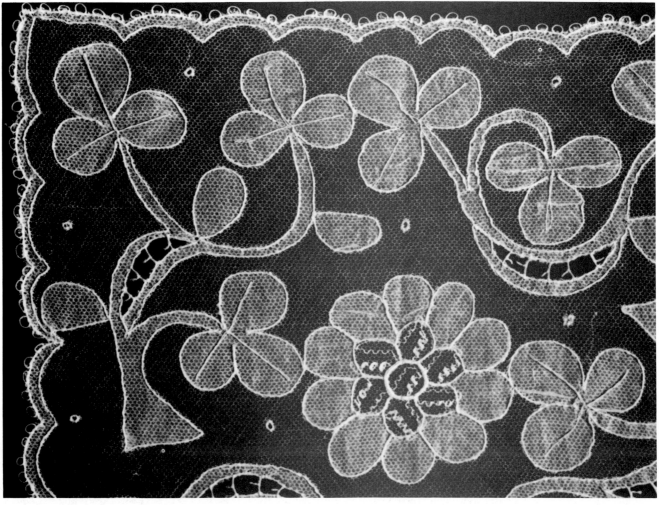

Tambour hook.

Tambour Lace

Tambour is a type of chain stitch embroidery that developed in the Far East where it was used for colorful embroideries in silk and wool for rugs, hangings, and garments. Tambour worked on fine white muslin with white thread became popular in Europe at the time of Louis XIV. The frames used to hold the work resembled tambour drums, so the frames, the hooks used to make the chain stitches, and the work were all called tambour. Tambour lace worked on fine machine-made net was made in England after 1820, especially in the town of Coggeshall in Essex and the Isle of Wight, and also in Limerick, Ireland. This type of lace is known by all of these place names. Originally, this lace was made on square or diamond mesh net, but later hexagonal mesh net was generally used.

A hook similar to a fine crochet hook is used to make the chain stitches. A screw on the side of the handle holds the straight-shafted hook in place and allows different sizes of hooks to be used to suit the thread. The screw also shows the worker which way the hook is facing so the net threads will not be caught accidentally.

The net is stretched on a frame. The hook is held above the frame and the thread below. The hook is pushed through the fabric and the thread wrapped around the hook, which then pulls a loop of thread up through the fabric and through the preceding loop, forming a chain stitch. Patterns are outlined and filled in with the chain stitch; finer thread may be used for the fillings to

Left: Sampler of tambour designs.

Below: Chain stitch on net.

give a more delicate appearance. Limerick tambour lace often includes needle-run fillings.

Tambour work is also done using special sewing machines that make chain stitches, with the fabric hand-guided.

Tambour chain stitch is also used to appliqué organdy or muslin to net.

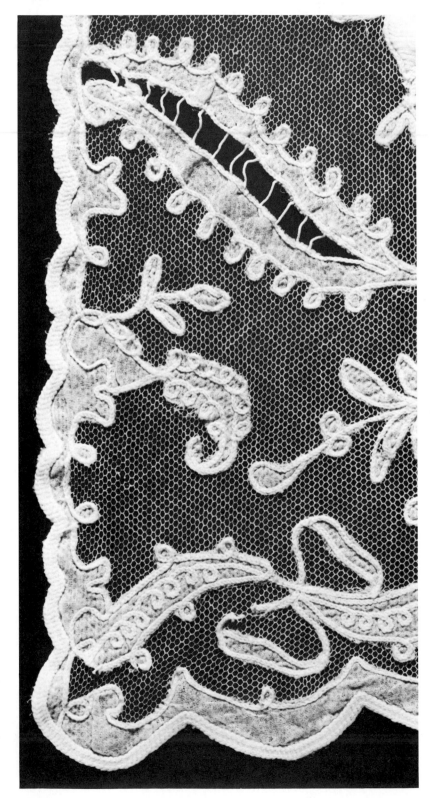

Detail of a lace curtain made by appliquéing muslin to fine net with chain stitch. Both the muslin and the net were cut out of the center of the leaf and needlework bars were added.

Needlework on Woven Fabric

Openwork embroidery on woven fabric developed in prehistoric times. Fine fabrics were woven in China, India, Mesopotamia, and Egypt thousands of years before the time of Christ. Remnants of fabrics found in the Nile Valley in Egypt have been dated as early as 5000 B.C. Fragments dating as early as 3000 B.C. have been found in Palestine. According to legend, the Chinese silk fabric industry was born during the twenty-seventh century B.C., when Empress Hsi-Ling-Shi discovered that silk filament could be unwound from the cocoons of the worms that were eating the leaves of the royal mulberry trees, after a cocoon accidentally dropped in her cup of tea.

Archaeologists have found clay tablets that had served as record books for Sumerian weavers in Mesopotamia dating as early as 2200 B.C. The Babylonians, who followed the Sumerians in dominating Mesopotamia around 1800 B.C., also placed great emphasis on weaving, but to them the art of embroidery was even more important. Their knowledge of embroidery spread to all the

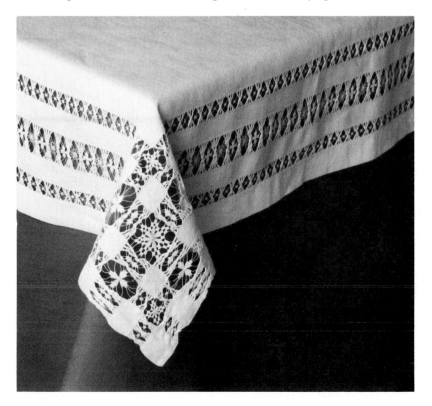

Elaborate needle-weaving designs fill the intersections of three drawnwork borders.

Mediterranean countries. The textile arts were highly prized in the Persian Empire, which by the sixth century B.C. reached from Greece and Egypt on the west to the borders of India on the east. Trade routes through Persia brought silks from China, cotton fabric from India, and Persian designs and techniques for textile arts to Europe.

Needlework originally was done to join and strengthen delicate woven fabrics and later developed into beautiful decoration. According to Greek mythology, a mortal named Arachne invented lace-embroidery, learning patterns from the spiders. She challenged Athena (goddess of warfare and wisdom, patroness of arts and crafts) to a weaving contest. After the contest, Athena changed the boastful Arachne into a spider so she could spend eternity perfecting her stitches. Another version of the myth says that Arachne became the first spider—the scientific name for spiders, *arachnid,* comes from her name.

In the Rig-Veda, the oldest of the sacred books of the Hindus, an invocation to the goddess of the full moon, Raka, expresses the hope that the goddess could sew with a never-breaking needle. This indicates the importance of needlework in early Indian history, and also that needles made of hand-beaten gold, copper, and bronze, or splinters of wood or bone were very fragile.

Cleopatra's robes were described by the Roman poet Lucan as having been made from skillfully woven Sidonian (Phoenician) fabric made transparent by embroidery done in Egypt.

European fabrics were not so filmy as the Eastern muslins, so embroiderers would sometimes draw out some of the fabric threads to give a lighter effect. This led to drawnwork borders on sacramental and burial robes, and eventually on clothing and household linens. Openwork, white-on-white embroideries were important parts of folk costumes and household articles throughout Europe, especially in the Scandinavian countries. Immigrants brought their traditional embroideries with them.

Young needleworkers in Europe and America learned embroidery stitches by making samplers. A sampler was not only a learning tool, but was also a record of the various stitches that could be referred to later. In addition to colorful designs and alphabets or quotations in cross-stitch and crewel embroidery, samplers from the colonial period often included openwork embroidery—eyelet, drawnwork, and fagoting. Some samplers consisted entirely of these stitches.

Openwork embroidery developed into needle lace, which in turn became the inspiration for more complex and beautiful openwork embroidery.

There are four general ways of making open spaces with lace embroidery on fabric:

1. Drawnwork—making an openwork pattern in fabric either by (a) removing some of the fabric threads and decorating the remaining threads with stitchery or (b) moving the fabric threads together by pulling the stitches tight

2. Eyelet embroidery—overcasting around holes punched or cut in the fabric

3. Cutwork—cutting out areas of fabric after the design shapes have been outlined with buttonhole stitches

4. Fagoting—openwork embroidery stitches connecting strips of fabric

Drawnwork

No simple, clear, descriptive names distinguish between making open embroidery designs by removing some of the fabric threads or by moving some of the fabric threads out of their original alignment by pulling the stitches tight. The first technique is often called *drawn threadwork,* because the threads are withdrawn. The second technique is called *drawn fabric* work in Britain and *pulled threadwork* in the United States. The names do not help much in differentiating between the two techniques because pull and draw in this sense have the same meaning—one pulls on a thread to draw it out of the fabric. Some authorities use the terms *withdrawn element* and *deflected element* (using *element* to mean threads of the fabric so the fabric threads and embroidery threads will not be confused). For most of us, these terms evoke a chemistry lab rather than lacy embroidery.

Sampler of drawnwork stitches, showing how fabric threads are pulled together to create open spaces.

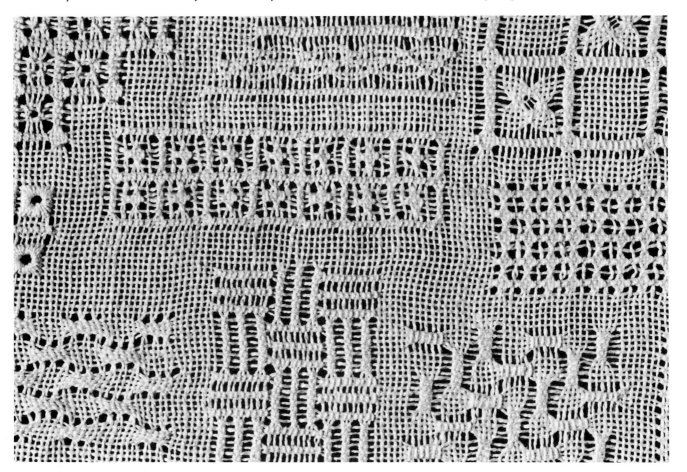

We are using the term *drawnwork* to include openwork embroidery made both by withdrawing some of the fabric threads and by drawing fabric threads together by pulling the stitches tight. This definition agrees with the suggestion made by Pat Earnshaw, author of *Dictionary of Lace*, to use a comprehensive term such as drawnwork to describe the creation of an openwork pattern in a textile, either by drawing threads out of the material in restricted areas or by drawing threads together so spaces are formed. The two techniques often occur together, and some of the same stitches are used in both. In some examples, it is difficult to tell if fabric threads have been removed or just moved. The cross threads remaining after some of the fabric threads have been removed are themselves moved into different alignment with decorative embroidery stitches. It seems appropriate to use drawnwork as a general name, which includes embroideries made by removing or moving some of the fabric threads.

Construction
Threads moved from original position

In this type of drawnwork, the sewing thread is pulled tight enough with some stitches that the fabric threads are moved from their original alignment, forming openwork patterns.

In eighteenth-century Britain and colonial America this type of drawnwork was done on fine cambric and was called *Dresden work,* for the city in eastern Germany. It was very popular in parts of Germany, where it was called *open stitchery,* in the Netherlands, where it is called *Persian openwork* (reflecting its historical background), and in Scandinavia. Exquisite pieces are also being made in the Philippine Islands, using extremely fine fabric.

The embroidery thread is usually the same color and thickness as the threads of the fabric. Placement of the stitches is determined by counting fabric threads. Openwork stitches are used primarily as fillings for design areas and occasionally as allover background. Areas of open stitchery are outlined with suitable embroidery stitches. Portions of the design may be embroidered with satin stitch or other flat filling stitches that do not pull the fabric threads together.

Construction
Threads removed from the fabric

In this type of drawnwork, some of the fabric threads are taken out of the fabric. The threads remaining in these borders or design areas are then decorated with needlework.

Rows of warp and weft threads are drawn out of the fabric. At the edges of the design areas, the sides of the open spaces where threads have been cut are overcast or buttonhole stitched, or the cut threads are woven back into the fabric for a short distance. Then hemstitching, twisting, knot stitches, needle-weaving, and

Drawnwork angel.

other decorative stitches are used to make lacy patterns with the remaining threads.

If both the warp and weft threads are removed, an open space is left where the threads crossed. Thread is secured diagonally, horizontally, and vertically across the space, crossing at the center. Wheels, spider webs, and woven flower or cross designs are worked on these "spoke" or "ray" threads. (This type of needlework developed into Tenerife lace.)

Hemstitching: Drawnwork borders are usually hemstitched along the top and bottom edges to secure the hem and to group the fabric threads.

Twisting: The needle brings the second group of threads back over the first group; the working thread holds the groups in position. There are numerous variations of the twist.

Needle weaving: The basic weaving stitch (in and out, back and forth) is worked over two or more groups of fabric threads in a border or over "spoke" threads in a space. A wide variety of patterns—flowers, crosses, birds, etc.—can be woven on the "spoke" threads.

Knot stitch: Wavy or straight lines of embroidery thread can be added by working knot stitches over the fabric threads. These threads often form the "spoke threads" for needle-weaving or other embroidery in spaces. Knot stitches are also used to tie groups of fabric threads into clusters or bundles. Spider webs and open wheels are made with knot stitches around intersecting "spoke" threads.

Woven wheels: Small woven wheels can be worked wherever the working thread crosses another thread. Larger wheels can be woven where several threads cross.

In some drawnwork borders or design areas, squares of solid fabric are left by alternately drawing out a given number of threads and leaving the same number in place in both directions. This makes a checkerboard pattern of open squares and threads alternating with threads and squares of intact fabric. The threads and the open spaces are then embroidered with knot stitches, woven wheels, or lace stitches.

Drawnwork stitches

1. Hemstitching.

2. Twisting the fabric threads remaining after the crosswise threads were withdrawn.

3. Needle weaving.

4. Knot stitch, which can be tied over single or multiple fabric threads.

5. Small woven wheels.

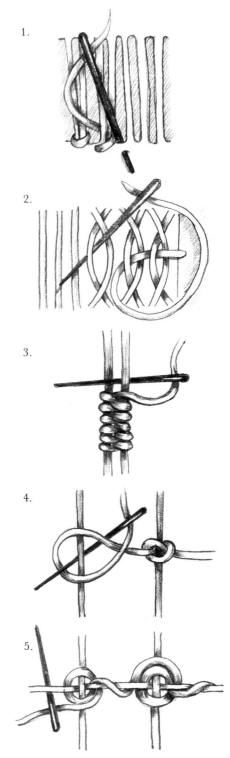

● Distinctive Features

1. Threads tied in clusters with knot stitches

2. Straight and wavy lines of thread added with knot stitches

3. Needle-woven designs such as flowers and crosses

4. Hemstitching

5. Corners where all fabric threads have been removed and edged with buttonhole stitches (sometimes with overcasting)

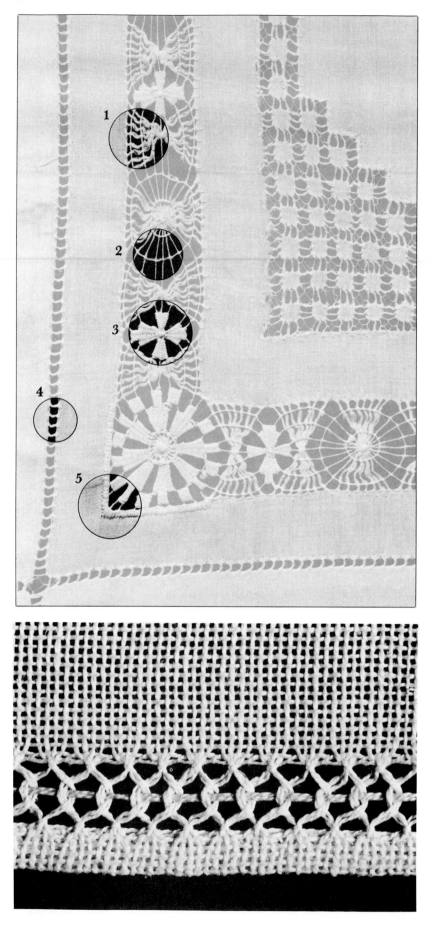

Drawnwork table scarf.

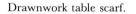

Drawnwork border, hemstitched and fabric threads twisted.

Groups of fabric threads were withdrawn in both directions from this handkerchief corner. The remaining threads were rearranged and the spaces filled with lace stitches.

Two borders of drawnwork decorate this petticoat flounce. The hem, lower border, and dividing lines are hemstitched. Curving lines of knot stitches make fans with the fabric threads in the lower border. In the upper border, alternately withdrawing and leaving groups of threads both horizontally and vertically made a checkerboard pattern. Overcasting and lace stitches rearranged the remaining fabric threads.

Hardanger

Hardanger is a distinctive type of counted-thread drawnwork named for the Hardanger district in southeastern Norway, where it was used extensively to decorate folk costumes and household linens. Immigrants brought the art to America. Traditionally, Hardanger was worked with white thread on white linen in geometric patterns. Since the 1970s there has been widespread interest in Hardanger, using all colors and imaginative designs, including religious symbols for church linens, monograms, and themes with personal significance.

Hardanger is characterized by blocks of satin stitch called kloster blocks, arranged to outline open spaces. The designs are based on squares of kloster blocks, open areas, open areas with lace stitches, and plain fabric, combined to make practically any design. Satin stitch and other surface embroidery is used to extend and complement the openwork design.

A typical kloster block consists of five stitches worked over four fabric threads. In horizontal and vertical rows, four threads are left between kloster blocks. In diagonal rows, the blocks are stitched alternately horizontally and vertically.

Within the design area, the fabric threads are cut and removed where opposing kloster blocks secure the thread ends.

The fabric threads remaining in the design area are then covered with needle weaving or overcasting, and some of the open squares are decorated with picots, wheels, lace stitch, or other fillings.

Satin stitch borders and designs are often added to fill in between and around openwork areas.

Right: Two strips of Hardanger were inset into this skirt.

Below: Diagram of a typical Hardanger motif, showing which threads are removed after the kloster blocks are stitched.

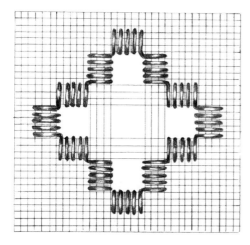

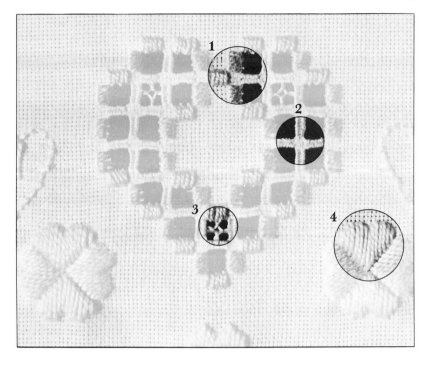

● Distinctive Features

1. Open areas bordered by satin stitch kloster blocks

2. Fabric threads in the openwork areas covered with needle weaving (or sometimes overcasting)

3. Decorative fillings in some open spaces

4. Satin stitch designs

Left: Hardanger heart motif with four-leaf clovers in satin stitch.

Below: Small Hardanger mat, worked as a diamond shape. Picots enhance the needle-woven bars in the center squares. Lace stitch decorates the middle row of open squares in the border.

Drawnwork Mesh

Several drawnwork techniques have the effect of making square mesh in woven fabric. *Overcast openwork* creates a square mesh by pulling groups of threads together by tightly overcasting around them. The area of the fabric in which the mesh is to be formed is outlined in buttonhole stitch or overcasting. With loosely woven fabric, mesh can be made without removing threads, by pulling groups of threads together with tight overcasting. With closely woven fabric, groups of threads in the design area are alternately removed and left in place (for example, two threads removed, two left in place). The remaining threads are wrapped (overcast) with sewing thread to strengthen the mesh and make the holes clear and distinct. If there is only one overcast stitch between the fabric thread intersections, the woven crossing of the fabric threads can be seen. On the back of the fabric, the overcasting stitches form a cross-stitch over the intersection.

A heavier mesh is made by working two stitches between the intersections and two stitches across the intersection.

Larger mesh are made by alternately removing and leaving four fabric threads. Four overcast stitches are made between intersections. The original weave of the fabric shows on the front at the intersections, with the overcast stitches crossing the intersections diagonally on the back.

Mesh made by any of these methods may then be decorated with designs woven into the mesh with darning stitch (filling

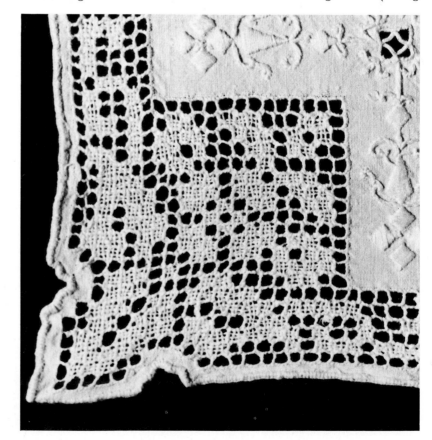

Filet tiré in the corner of a tablecloth. The mesh was made throughout the openwork area and the design then worked in cloth stitch over the mesh as in net darning. The edges of the openwork areas were overcast. There is a strip of the original fabric between the openwork and the buttonhole stitched outer edge of the cloth.

threads going across the squares) or with cloth stitch (filling threads going up and down and across the squares), as in net darning. This type of embroidery was called *filet tiré*. The design area was usually an integral part of the fabric from which the tablecloth or other article was made, but sometimes borders or medallions were made separately and then joined to the article being decorated.

An effect similar to filet tiré is obtained by forming the mesh only in the background areas, leaving all the fabric threads in their original positions in the design areas. This type of work was called *mosaic work*. In *Russian drawnwork* the design areas are outlined in chain stitch.

Rhodes work gives an effect similar to overcast openwork, but the result is heavier. The "four-sided," or "punched," stitch is used, working with a thick needle to push the threads apart. The stitches form a cross-stitch on the back. They are pulled tight to make holes in the fabric. The residual cloth in the design is decorated with surface embroidery, usually satin stitch.

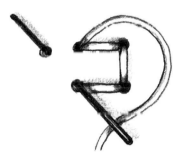

Four-sided stitch (or punch stitch) is worked with a thick needle to form the mesh for Rhodes work.

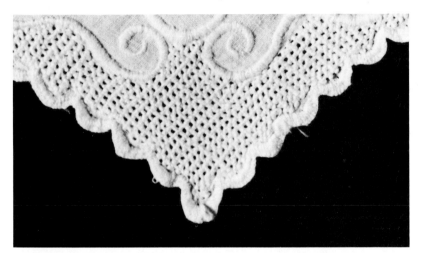

Left: A collar with Rhodes work mesh, satin stitch swirls, and buttonhole stitch scalloped edging.

Below: Mosaic work table mat. The mesh was made only in the background, leaving the original fabric in the design areas.

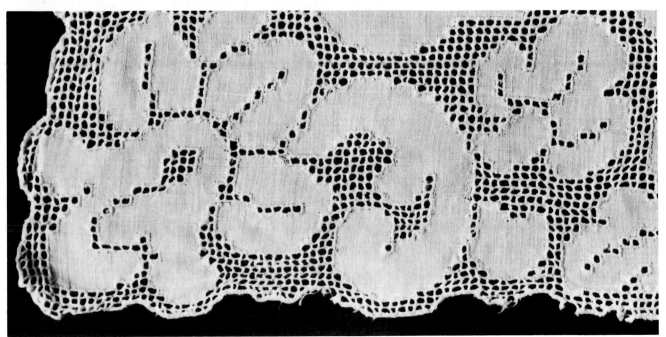

Eyelet Embroidery

Eyelet embroidery designs are formed with open ovals, circles, and teardrop shapes. The eyelets are outlined with small running stitches and then cut or punched with a stiletto and closely overcast. Edges of the work are finished with scallops, which are buttonhole stitched.

Eyelet embroidery was used extensively in the late eighteenth and in the nineteenth centuries for clothing and household linens. The entire design was made of eyelets of various sizes. Newer designs include leaves and petals, outlines and stems in satin, outline, and buttonhole stitch, and may include ladder work— narrow strips of cutwork crossed by bars that are buttonhole stitched or overcast.

Eyelet embroidery is also called *Broderie Anglaise* (English embroidery). *Madeira work* is eyelet embroidery made on the Portuguese island by that name off the coast of Morocco. Eyelet embroidery is usually white-on-white, but Madeira work is characteristically done with light blue or gray thread on white fabric.

The eyelet edgings, insertions, and allover patterns available commercially, sometimes called *Swiss work*, are made with Schiffli embroidery machines, which are described in Machine-made Lace (page 143).

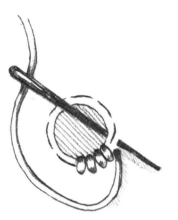

Above: An eyelet being made. Overcasting stitches are worked over small running stitches around the hole.

Below: Eyelet embroidery on a table scarf. Round eyelets form a scalloped border and teardrop shaped eyelets form flowers.

Compass Work

A special type of eyelet embroidery consists of circles over-lapped in such a manner that four petal shapes are formed around each circle. This is called *compass, thimble,* or *spool work,* depending upon what implement was used to draw the circles. These designs were used for yokes and sleeves, collars and cuffs, baby clothes, blouses, pillows, and household linens as allover design motifs and insertions or edgings.

After running stitches were worked around the petal shapes, the openings were cut and buttonhole stitched. The openings were sometimes filled with lace stitches, or bobbinet was sewed behind them. The centers of the circles might be embroidered with a cross, star, or other design.

Another variation of compass work started with circles touching rather than overlapping. A cross was cut in each circle nearly to the point where one circle touched the adjoining one. The fabric was folded to the back and the arcs buttonhole stitched. The resulting open squares were then filled in with woven wheels or other lace stitches.

Above: Patterns for compass work eyelet embroidery designs built up with overlapping circles.

Left: Compass work eyelet embroidery on a guest towel.

Ayrshire Work

Ayrshire work is a delicate type of needlework popular in the middle 1800s that combined eyelet embroidery and drawnwork with surface embroidery.

At the close of the Napoleonic wars (1815), changing dress styles called for lacy embroidery with more body than the sheer tamboured muslin or Dresden drawn thread work that had been in vogue. A thriving cottage industry developed around Ayr in southwestern Scotland. Embroidered floral designs combined satin stitch, outline stitch, eyelets, and openwork areas filled with lace stitches, drawnwork, or net darning. Cotton manufacturers printed designs on muslin, using carved wooden blocks or rollers and water soluble blue dye. The printed material was sent to workers, called flowerers, in the surrounding area and in Ireland. The completed embroidery was returned to be laundered and marketed, either as made-up articles or ready to be made up by the purchaser, chiefly for baby dresses and caps, frills for caps and shirts, and wide collars and cuffs.

By the latter part of the 1800s, Swiss embroidery machines had largely replaced the hand embroiderers. Similar work is still done in the Philippines and China.

Ayrshire-type embroidery on a baby dress made in the Philippines.

Cutwork

Cutwork embroidery produces a lacy effect because parts of the design or background are cut out. The design is first outlined with running stitches, which are then covered with closely worked buttonhole stitches. The corded edge of the stitches is on the side that will be cut away. In simple cutwork, the open spaces are small. As designs become more elaborate with larger cutout areas, bars are added to strengthen the work and keep the solid areas in place. These bars, which may be straight or branched, are covered with buttonhole stitches. Spider webs and woven wheels are also used for support and decoration. *Richelieu cutwork* is more open and lacy, with picots on the bars.

Left: Buttonhole stitch bars form six-pointed stars in the background of the cutwork design on this blouse.

Below: Cutwork in progress. Buttonhole stitches are being made over running stitches outlining the design. The areas marked with Xs will be cut away.

An older type of cutwork, often called *Italian cutwork,* is closely related to drawnwork. The edges of the design area are buttonhole stitched, then threads are secured across the area to form the framework for the designs, which are built up with buttonhole stitches. The designs are usually geometric.

The 1902 Sears, Roebuck and Co. catalog had nearly a page of shams, table covers, scarves, tidies, and doilies in "Spachtel or Irish Point work" with openwork designs "tamboured on best

Cutwork embroidery decorates these kid leather gloves.

quality lawn." These were imported, made by "expert European operators." Needlework magazines of the period included directions for doing Spachtel work by hand. It was described as a type of cutwork in which the pattern is outlined with a single or double row of chain-stitch. The cutout areas of the work contained some twisted bars and lace stitches. This was not a durable type of cutwork because the chain stitches tend to pull away from the fabric when laundered.

Crocheted and tatted medallions were sometimes inserted into collars, table linens, and similar articles to give the effect of cutwork embroidery.

The design in the corner of this napkin features ladder work—long narrow open areas of cutwork crossed by straight bars. The center motif is built up with buttonhole stitches (needle lace). The edging is net darning.

A crocheted medallion was inserted to give the effect of Italian cutwork in this doily.

Left: Spachtel cutwork. The design was worked in chain stitch (made either with a tambour hook or a chain stitch sewing machine), with some areas cut out and threads sewed across the spaces.

Below: Cutwork flowers and leaves around a small mat.

Hedebo

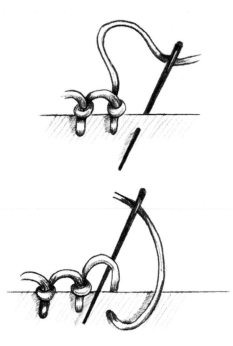

Above: Hedebo buttonhole stitch is worked in two steps, resulting in a little knot at the top of the stitch.

Below: Loops of thread covered with Hedebo buttonhole stitches make the triangles in this edging.

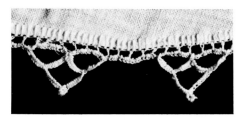

Right: Hedebo motifs feature rounded cut-out spaces like these leaves and ovals, with decorative fillings. Rings of Hedebo buttonhole stitch make the edging.

Hedebo is a form of cutwork embroidery that originated among the peasants who lived ("bo") on the heath ("Heden") near Copenhagen, Denmark. It was originally used to decorate men's shirts, women's clothing, and household linens. Prior to 1850, Hedebo embroidery consisted of conventionalized floral designs with drawnwork in the leaves and petals, which were outlined with double rows of chain stitch. After 1850 designs changed to cutout, rounded spaces, such as circles, ovals, crescents, hearts, teardrops, and long leaves, arranged in patterns.

The open spaces are filled with lace stitches. Sprigs of small leaves and flowers worked in satin stitch complete the designs. A variant of the buttonhole stitch is used to outline the shapes and to work some of the fillings and the characteristic edgings (sometimes called *Danish lace*), which finish the articles.

The distinguishing feature of the Hedebo buttonhole stitch is a little knot at the top of the vertical stitch. It is worked in two steps.

The design shapes are outlined with running stitches. Then the fabric is cut from the center of the shape to the edge, at short enough intervals so the cloth can be turned back to the wrong side along the stitched line. The Hedebo buttonhole stitch is worked over the folded edge and then the extra fabric is trimmed away from the back.

The open areas are filled with lace stitches, especially triangles built up of Hedebo buttonhole stitch, twisted buttonhole stitch, and woven wheels.

Edgings are made with loops, triangles, and rings of Hedebo and twisted buttonhole stitch.

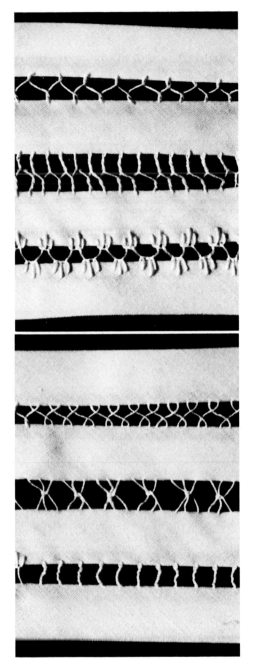

Fagoting

Using openwork embroidery stitches to join pieces of fabric produces lacy effects. This type of embroidery is called *insertion work* or *fagoting.* It was popular in colonial America and has been used since that time for delicate trimmings.

The pieces of fabric to be joined are first hemmed, then basted to a piece of paper with a uniform distance between each (usually from 1/4 to 1/2 inch). Any of a variety of stitches can be worked between the fabric pieces, bridging the space between them.

Above: Samplers of fagoting stitches

    Crisscross fagoting

    Twisted insertion stitch

    Grouped buttonhole stitches

    Herringbone stitch

    Fagot bundle

    Bar fagoting

Left: Collar made by joining strips of ribbed fabric with fagoting. The edging is Irish crochet.

Needle Lace

Needle lace is "stitches in air" made on a framework of threads rather than on fabric. Needle lace was considered to be the finest, most aristocratic (and most expensive) of the laces so highly prized by royalty and churchmen from the time of Columbus until the industrial revolution in the mid-1800s.

The earliest type of needle lace is *Reticella*. It developed from cutwork embroidery and is sometimes called *Italian cutwork*. Reticella is made by drawing out threads from a piece of fabric, leaving only a few carefully spaced threads to form the framework of the design. These threads and others, which are added to form diagonals, are wrapped in figure-eight fashion with the working thread. The designs are worked over these threads with variations of the buttonhole stitch.

Eventually, needleworkers found that they did not need to start with a fabric. They could work the same designs and many others on frameworks of threads basted to a parchment backing. When the lace was finished, the basting threads were removed and the lace was free of the parchment. The technique was not limited to geometric designs in square grids because the supporting threads could outline any shape on the parchment backing, allowing far more freedom and variety in the designs.

Different lacemaking regions developed their own characteristic designs and stitch variations. The resulting laces were usually named for the geographic area in which they were made. Although the stitches were all variations of the buttonhole stitch, great variety was obtained by changing the size of the loops and spacing, adding extra twists, and so on. Certain design themes were characteristic of each type of lace.

The various steps in making needle lace were done by different workers—one would sew the background mesh, another would fill in a solid area, another would work a heavy outline around a design area, and so on. Ten different workers might have been involved in making one piece of lace. This division of work promoted efficiency because each worker became very proficient at one stitch, and it also prevented workers from taking all the secrets of making that particular type of lace with them if they moved to another area.

In museums and historic costume collections are examples of the magnificent needle laces made in the sixteenth to eighteenth

Making needle lace. Outlining thread is basted to the pattern. Design areas are filled with appropriate filling stitches, most of which are variations of the buttonhole stitch. Outline threads are then closely covered with buttonhole stitches. Removing the basting stitches frees the lace from the pattern.

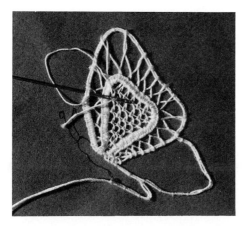

centuries. The stitches of *gros point de Venise* were built up to produce a three-dimensional effect that looked like carved ivory. Brussels *point de gaze* is filmy and delicate. Lace identification books will help identify these and many other types of needle lace, but you are unlikely to find them in your trunks and attics. The pieces of needle lace that you are likely to find were probably imported from Europe or the Orient since 1900. Needle lace designs for edgings, collars, and so on have been reproduced as chemical laces made with the Schiffli machines for over one hundred years.

Construction

Two strands of outlining thread are basted to a paper or cloth pattern. The design areas are filled in with variations of the buttonhole stitch, which can create solid areas, raised details, openwork patterns, or delicate mesh. The outline threads are closely buttonhole stitched. When the work is completed, the basting stitches are removed and the lace is free of the background.

The stitches used to make needle lace are also used to make lace with premade tapes and needlework. This is described in Battenberg Lace (page 122).

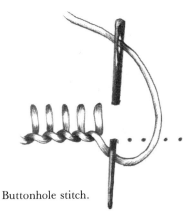

Buttonhole stitch.

Needle lace mat with a floral pattern.

● Distinctive Features

Buttonhole stitches form:

1. Bars, straight or curved, often with picots

2. Patterned areas

3. Solid outlines

Opposite page: Table mat of needle lace made in an Italian convent, c. 1930. (Complete mat is shown on page 158.)

Right: Variations of buttonhole stitch used in needle lace (and in Battenberg, see page 122).

Below right: Triangle of needle lace with a geometric pattern.

Below: Insertion of point de gaze needle lace in Belgium Duchesse bobbin lace. The mesh background was made with single buttonhole stitches. The central petals of the flowers were made separately and sewed in place to give added dimension.

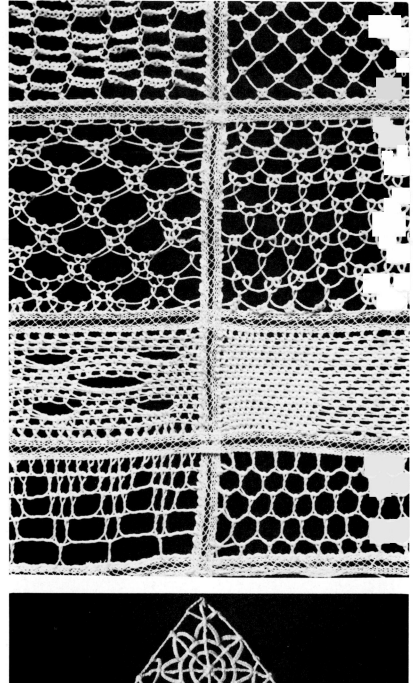

weaving, and the spokes were grouped and regrouped with knot stitches.

This type of lace was especially popular in Spain in the sixteenth and seventeenth centuries. It was brought to the Western Hemisphere by the conquistadors and missionaries. Tenerife is named for the largest of the Canary Islands off the northwest coast of Africa because that island is famous for this type of lace. A similar but much filmier lace is made in Paraguay called *nanduti* (from a native Indian word for "web"). The basic technique is the same as for Tenerife lace, but nanduti is worked with finer threads and more delicate designs.

Construction

Individual motifs in Tenerife lace are usually circular, but they may be ovals, squares, diamonds, stars, or other shapes. Individual motifs are usually fairly small because larger ones must have more threads crossing at the center, which makes a lump. Small motifs are joined to form larger articles.

The spokes, which form the basis of a motif, are made by taking thread across the center from successive opposite points on the circumference. Metal or plastic forms, pins in a firm pad, or support stitches on heavy paper or on cloth held in a frame are used to hold the spoke threads. Designs are then worked with needle and thread. The center is often a woven or back-stitched wheel, and the rays or petals are worked by weaving over and under a given number of spokes. Other types of designs are made by tying groups of spokes together using knot stitches.

The Tenerife lace technique of fastening threads across an area and then working needle-weaving and knot stitch designs over the spoke threads has been used to make the centers of crocheted, tatted, and hairpin lace motifs, and to fill in the open spaces between circular motifs.

Tenerife braid is closely related to Tenerife lace, but it is made in strips, and its framework threads are parallel to one another rather than crossed in the center. In the early 1900s Tenerife braid could be purchased ready-made in needlework shops, or it could be made on special forms available with straight edges or with scalloped or V edges. After the framework threads were wound back and forth across the form, being caught on pegs or in notches, designs were worked along one edge with needle weaving and knot stitch. The loops along the other edge could be drawn together to form circular motifs, either by bringing the loops together in the center or by forming an open circle into which a center motif was worked by crochet or needlework.

Tenerife braid was also used to make insertions and edgings. Needle weaving and knot stitch designs were worked across the width of the form, making a lace that closely resembled drawnwork embroidery.

The Tenerife lace technique was also used to make shaped

Above: Looms for making Tenerife lace. The top two have retractable metal prongs on which the spoke threads are wound. Either round or square motifs can be made on the plastic circle; spoke threads are held with support stitches sewed into the holes.

Below: Working the design of a Tenerife lace motif on spoke threads taken back and forth through a circle of support stitches sewed into thin cardboard.

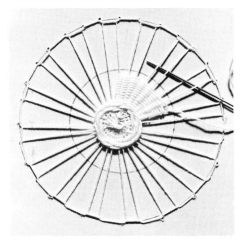

articles such as collars and baby bonnets (the crown and brim were made separately). The shapes were drawn on cardboard and pins or support stitches placed to hold the spoke threads.

Tenerife embroidery is similar to the lace, except that the spoke threads are sewed into the fabric that is being decorated. The design is worked on the spoke threads without going into the background fabric.

● Distinctive Features

1. Spoke threads crossing at the center of the motif

2. Petals and other designs made with needle weaving

3. Spoke threads held in position with knot stitches

4. Small motifs joined to form larger ones

Tenerife mat with four-petaled flowers in the larger center motif and in each of the ten small motifs around it.

A Tenerife motif forms the center of this tatted star.

Above: This little mat, made in the early 1900s, has a different design in each of the seven motifs around the fabric center, which was decorated with drawnwork. The outer edge of the Tenerife motif was finished with shells of buttonhole stitch.

Left: Woven diamonds and double-curving rows of knot stitch make a dainty pattern in the center motif of this Tenerife doily. The motifs in the outer row are D-shaped to fit along the edge of the center motif.

Variations

The general technique used in making Tenerife lace has been used in a number of crafts. Ornamental buttons are made by buttonhole stitching around bone, metal, or plastic rings, fastening spoke threads across the ring, and working needle-weaving designs on the spokes. These needle-woven buttons have traditionally been used on smocked garments. Making these buttons (and others) was a staple industry in Dorset, England, from before 1700 to about 1860. Needle-woven buttons are called *Dorset cross wheels, cartwheels, honeycombs,* and *spider web* buttons.

Ring work was popular in the early 1900s for making napkin rings, picture frames, purses, and similar articles. Single crochet or buttonhole stitches were worked around bone or metal rings. Spoke threads were fastened across the rings and designs worked on them, just as for crosswheel buttons. The rings were then sewed or crocheted together. Sometimes the spaces between the rings were also filled with needle-weaving designs.

The openwork motifs often included in pine-needle baskets are a form of Tenerife lace. These are worked with raffia on metal or plastic rings.

Flower medallions made on gadgets with names such as Flower Loom, Wonder Wheel, or Daisy Maker are related to Tenerife lace, but the emphasis is on the loops made by the spoke threads rather than on lace designs worked on the spoke threads. The flowers are generally made with yarn and are joined to make afghans and shawls. Individual medallions made of yarn or ribbon straw (synthetic raffia) are used to decorate sweaters, tote bags, and similar accessories, and to make designs on wall hangings. Usually there is one row of stitches, which may be of a contrasting color, around the center, either making a raised center or pulling the threads apart enough to make an open center. Looms for making these flowers are available in several sizes of circles, squares, and triangles.

Tenerife braid is made by working needle-weaving and knot stitch designs on stretched threads, but the threads are parallel instead of crossing in the center of a motif.

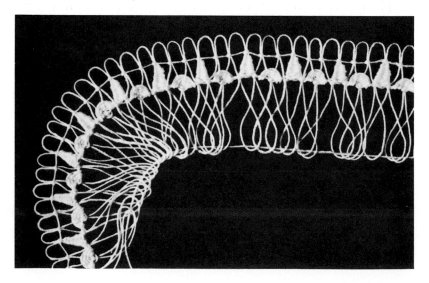

Dorset crosswheel buttons are made on bone, metal, or plastic rings, using the Tenerife lace technique to make the designs.

Pine needle baskets often include Tenerife motifs worked in raffia.

Flower medallions made of yarn are related to Tenerife lace, but the spoke threads form the petals instead of being the framework for lace designs.

Battenberg Lace

Battenberg is one of the many names applied to lace made with straight tapes and needlework stitches. Its origins go back to the development of bobbin lace and needle lace in the fifteenth and sixteenth centuries. Some lace patterns consisted of narrow strips winding through mesh backgrounds or doubling back and forth with the curves connected to each other. The background mesh or joinings were made as the strips were being made, or

Battenberg lace edges a curtain panel and a small tablecloth from the early 1900s.

sometimes the background or connections were made later, either with bobbins or needles. Attractive lace could also be made using straight tapes gathered to form curves or folded to make sharp corners. Straight tapes could be made much more rapidly than intricately curved ones, so the laces could be made more quickly. Machine-made tapes were among the earliest products of the industrial revolution. As these tapes became readily and inexpensively available, lacemakers were freed from the chore of making the tape, and this type of lacemaking became a popular pastime. In the middle of the nineteenth century it was called *modern point lace*. A 1902 publication called it simply *modern lace*.

The term *royal Battenberg lace* was given by Sara Hadley (a lace designer in New York who later became an editor of the *Ladies' Home Journal*) to a piece of lace that she exhibited at the Chicago World's Fair in 1893. Two royal weddings during the 1880s, which had great impact on the world of fashion and society, involved the princely family from Battenberg, a small principality in west central Germany. In 1884 Prince Louis of Battenberg married Victoria, granddaughter of Queen Victoria, and in 1885 Prince Henry of Battenberg married Beatrice, Queen Victoria's youngest daughter. Royal Battenberg lace differed from other laces made with tape and needlework because its background consisted of buttonholed bars with picots made by wrapping the thread twelve times around the needle. When twisted bars were used instead of the more time-consuming buttonholed bars and picots, the lace was called *Renaissance lace*. The terms Battenberg

Battenberg lace forms this American eagle, made in the early 1900s for a pillow cover eighteen inches square.

Above: Tapes used for Battenberg lace.

Below: Premade tape is basted to a pattern, gathered or folded to fit curves and corners. The spaces are filled with decorative stitches.

and Renaissance were soon used interchangeably.

If two or more kinds of tape were used, the lace was called *princess*. At least one of the tapes would have openwork in it, and often a tape with leaflike sections was used. Sometimes the term "princess" was used for laces made by sewing the tapes to machine-made net.

Many names have been used for these laces in different localities, each locality using different tapes or special stitches, but Battenberg is the name most commonly used in America. Another name in current use is *Brussels lace.*

In America in the early 1900s, a wide variety of patterns were available for Battenberg lace. The patterns were often stamped on green or pink muslin. The pattern stated the number of yards of tape needed and usually suggested filling stitches to use. Tablecloths, dresser and piano scarves, centerpieces and doilies, curtains and bedspreads, picture hats, parasol covers, collars and yokes, blouses and skirts, petticoats, and even baby bibs were all decorated with Battenberg. Entire garments, such as jackets, skirts, and dresses, were made of it.

The tape was usually machine-made, but bobbin lace, crocheted, macrame, and hairpin lace strips were also used. Many styles and widths of machine-made tape were available.

In addition to the straight tapes, various patterns of "leaf" tape, sometimes called *Honiton lace braid,* were available. These had alternate wide and narrow sections; some had dainty openwork fillings. Flower patterns could be made with two rows of leaf tape. One row would go up, across, down, across; the second row would cross between the leaves of the first row.

Many Battenberg patterns from the early 1900s included rings, often used as grapes or flower centers. These rings were made by wrapping thread a number of times around a pencil, finger, or dowel of suitable size and then buttonhole stitching or crocheting tightly over the threads. These rings could be purchased ready-made at stores that sold the patterns and tape. The 1902 Sears Roebuck catalog offered white and ecru linen rings and black silk rings in several sizes. White rings a half-inch in diameter cost three cents a dozen; the same size in black silk cost ten cents a dozen (plus two cents postage).

Construction

A premade tape is basted to a cloth or paper pattern. The tape crosses over itself, and is gathered to fit around curves and folded at corners and sharp turns to follow the pattern. The spaces are then filled with a variety of needle lace stitches, mostly variations of the buttonhole stitch, without stitching into the pattern. When the needlework is completed, the basting stitches are removed and the lace is free of the pattern.

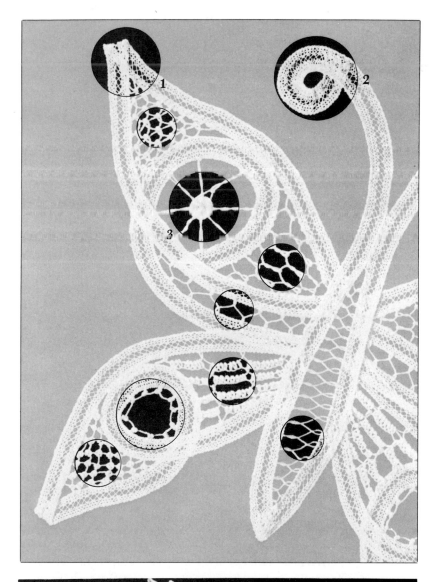

Battenberg lace butterfly.

Distinctive Features

1. Tape folded at corners and sharp turns

2. Tape gathered to fit curves

3. Needle weaving

Variations of buttonhole stitch (seven were used in this butterfly)

Rings made by wrapping thread many times around a dowel or finger and then buttonhole stitching over the threads were included in many Battenberg designs. The tape used in this doily has picots along one edge. Only two filling stitches were used.

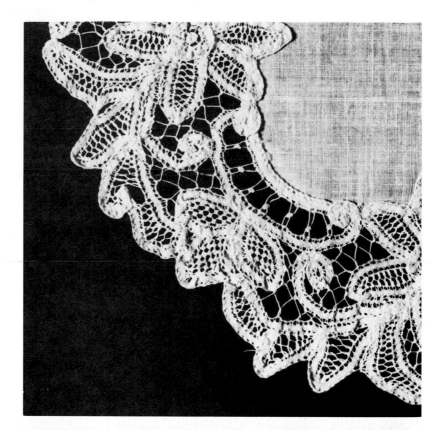

Right: The Battenberg lace edging on this small mat was made with narrow tape and five filling stitches.

Below: At least twenty-four filling stitches were used in making this delicate Battenberg lace collar.

Left: This narrow collar was made with heavier tape. Only two buttonhole stitch variations were used, but many needle-woven patterns were included.

Below: Leaf tape makes floral patterns around a center of Honiton bobbin lace in this small mat. A tape with picots on one side was used for the edging.

Novelty Tapes

Various forms of machine-made novelty tapes and cords were used in making decorative openwork fabrics, which were very popular in the early 1900s, especially in America. These tapes and cords were included in edgings, doilies, medallions, and collars to produce effects that could not be achieved by crocheting, tatting, or sewing alone. By using these tapes and cords the worker could complete a given area of work more quickly.

Rickrack tape was the first novelty tape to be manufactured, and it is still popular today.

Medallion tape and coronation cord used with crocheting and tatting were popular around 1920. Coronation cord was also used in embroidery work.

Tubular cord was hardly a novelty cord, since it was made to be used as corset strings, but sewing it into decorative openwork mats was a novel use.

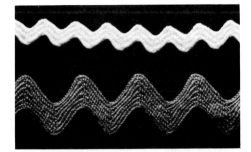

Rickrack

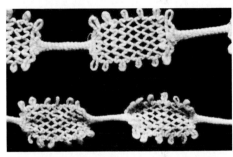

Medallion Tape

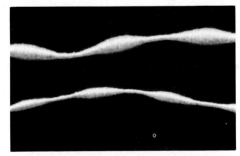

Coronation Cord

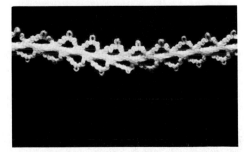

Picot Tape

Rickrack

Rickrack is the best known of the novelty tapes used in making lacy decorations. Before rickrack tape was manufactured with its flat zigzags woven in, *rickrack work* was done with straight tape. Diagonal lines of tiny running stitches were sewed back and forth across the tape; these were then pulled up to form three-dimensional triangles. The triangle points were drawn together to make rosettes, which sometimes had crocheted centers and edgings, or were sewn together to make other patterns.

Some designs, incorporating machine-made rickrack with crochet, had only enough crocheting to hold the rickrack in position; other designs were mostly crochet with only a little rickrack to add variety to the design. Tatting was also used with rickrack, but less commonly. Motifs and edgings were also made with rickrack and needlework.

Narrow rickrack and needlework make a lacy insertion and edging on an apron.

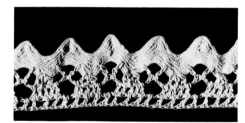

Edging made with wide rickrack and crochet.

Insertion made with two colors of rickrack, twisted together to make a "cable," with crochet.

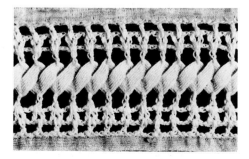

Medallion Tape

Another novelty tape used with tatting and crochet in the 1920s was medallion tape. A delightful and descriptive name for this tape was *turtle back braid*. It consisted of oval sections approximately twice as long as they are wide, with lattice centers and picot edges, alternating with thin straight sections. The tape was made in several widths. The picots or straight sections were caught with crochet or tatting stitches. This tape added openwork areas with a pattern that differed from the patterns made with the crochet or tatting stitches.

A similar tape currently available is called *Cluny tape*.

An edging with two straight strips of medallion tape and crochet.

A doily edging with medallion tape and tatting.

Picot Tape

Tapes consisting of a central cord with picot loops or open triangles along the edges were combined with tatting or crochet to create special effects.

An edging made with open-triangle novelty tape and crochet.

Coronation Cord

Coronation cord has alternating thin and thick sections. Fibers were wound around the core threads to make the thickness gradually increase and decrease. The thick portions were called loops and the thin sections stems. The cord was available as small, medium, and large, depending on the length and thickness of the loops. The cord was bent at the thin sections and caught with crochet or tatting stitches to form flower shapes, or to enhance an edging or insertion. Some articles had only enough crochet or tatting to hold the coronation cord together.

Coronation cord was also used in embroidery, sewed along a line as a border or stem, as flower petals, or as an outline, imitating the time-consuming padded satin stitch.

Right: This small bag was made of coronation cord and crochet. (The edging on the handkerchief is tatted.)

Below right: Doily edging of coronation cord and crochet.

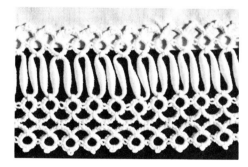

Above: Edging and rosettes made with small coronation cord and crochet.

Below: Edging of coronation cord and tatting.

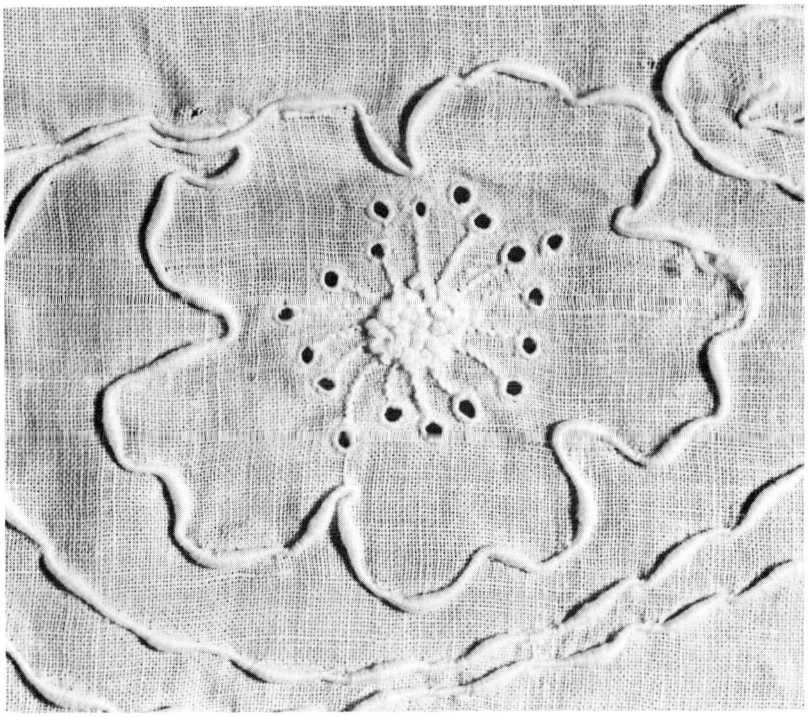

Coronation cord sewed to a doily to look like padded satin stitch. French knots, stem stitch, and eyelets complete the flowers.

Tubular Cord

The tubular cord used for corset strings (sometimes called *staylacing*) was used to make decorative table mats, hot dish mats, and so on in the early 1900s. The cord was sewed into circles (usually double circles to reduce the number of ends that had to be finished off) and flowers. Three- and four-strand braids and Solomon's or true love knots were sewed around and between the circles and flowers.

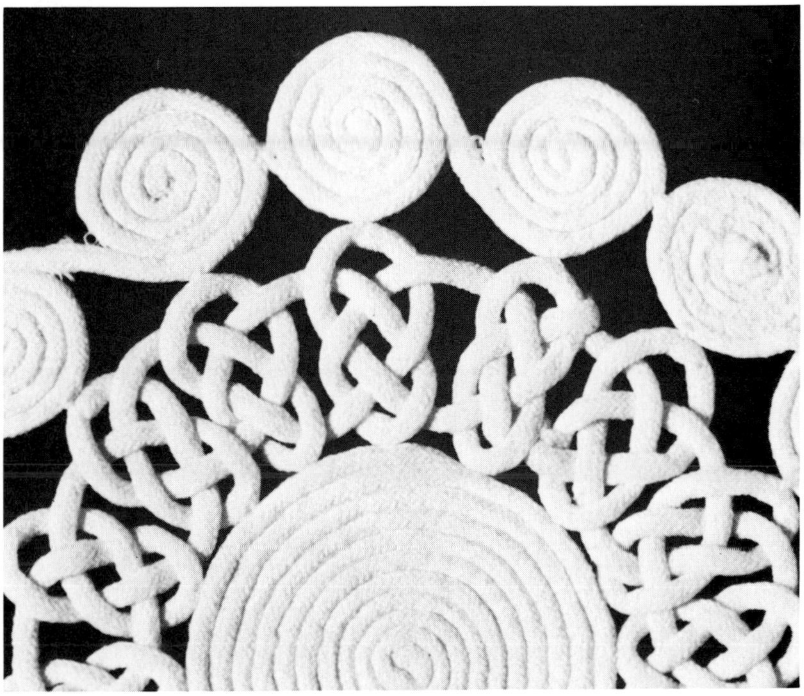

Corset cord mat with double circles and Solomon's or true love knots.

Machine-made Lace

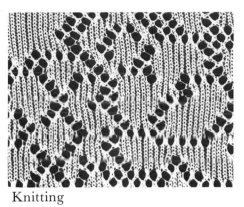

Knitting

Many people think of machine-made lace as being fairly new and somehow inferior to handmade lace. Neither assumption is necessarily true. Lacy fabrics were being made by machine over two hundred years ago. Better design and workmanship can be found in some machine-made laces than in their handmade counterparts.

The ingenuity of the inventors who developed lacemaking machines, and the skill and labor involved in creating machine-made lace deserve our respect and admiration. A design must be translated into punch cards or computer programs that take into account the number of bobbins or needles, the speed at which the machine moves, and the types of thread to be used.

Resembling Net Darning

Although in general machine-made laces are less expensive than those made by hand, this is not always true. Lacemakers in China and other parts of the Orient work for such extremely low wages that a piece of their handmade lace might cost less than pieces machine made in Europe or America.

The first machine-made nets were produced in the 1760s by a looping process that closely resembles hand knitting. Machines that made lace by twisting and braiding threads were developed early in the 1800s. Making lace and lacy fabrics with machine embroidery came a little later. By the middle of the 1800s, machine-made laces had largely replaced their handmade bobbin and needle lace counterparts. Reproductions became more accurate.

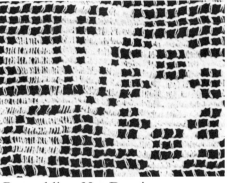

Embroidery on Net

There was a considerable amount of handwork in finishing some of the machine-made lace: "floats" (loose threads carried from one part of the design to another) were cut off by hand; cordonnets (heavy outlining threads) were run in by hand on some machine-made laces; and details were sometimes worked by hand with needle lace stitches to create special effects. New types of lace appeared, combining machine-made net with handwork. Workers embroidered and appliquéd designs on net in their homes as cottage industries and in factory workshops. Women who had the

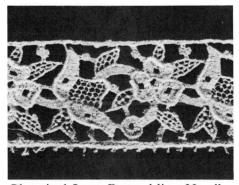

Chemical Lace Resembling Needle Lace

leisure to make lace as a pastime used machine-made net, tapes, and braids to simplify the process.

One of the earliest forerunners of the industrial revolution was the knitting frame invented in 1589 by the Reverend William Lee in England. Lee conceived the idea of a machine that could knit a whole row at once rather than one stitch at a time as in hand knitting. He also overcame the technical problems of working with weak, irregular thread, shaping the needles (which had their tips bent back so they could be pushed into grooves filed in the shafts of the needles) with minimal tools, working with low quality steel (which had to be toughened to retain elasticity and withstand pressure and tension), and lack of financial support. Although he eventually refined his machine so it had sixteen needles to the inch and could knit silk stockings, the machine was not commercially successful during Lee's lifetime. However, in the ten years after his death in 1610, the industry developed so rapidly that stocking frame workers organized a trade association.

For nearly two hundred years the stocking frame was used

This "shadow lace" shawl is machine-knitted lace.

only for plain knitting, making stockings and other garments. In the latter part of the eighteenth century, hand-knit hosiery with ribs and openwork patterns became fashionable. Fashions in lace favored light, airy mesh. Inventors trying to duplicate the fancy stitches of hand knitting and the fine uniform lace mesh benefitted from developments in related fields, particularly from spinning machines that could produce fine uniform cotton thread, and from improved steel and tools to shape it. Lack of money, patent infringements, and opposition (often violent) of hand workers who feared that machines would eliminate their livelihood were constant impediments to inventors. Shoddy workmanship, poor quality control, and competition from foreign machine lace industries (some of which developed from machines smuggled out of England) plagued the industrialists who invested in the machines. Nonetheless, new inventions and modifications mechanized the lacemaking industry.

Sewing machines for home use stimulated the demand for inexpensive machine-made lace to create styles like this dress from the early 1900s.

Knitting Machines

The stocking frame was adapted to knit openwork patterns in hosiery in the mid-1700s. By the 1770s machines produced very fine silk *point net,* so called because the points of wire hooks selected and transferred the loops to make the pattern. These machines, like the stocking frame, had a needle for each loop, and they made horizontal rows of loops with a continuous thread. Like hand knitting, the rows would "run" or unravel if a thread broke or was cut.

The Warp Frame machine was developed in 1775. Like the stocking frame, it had a needle for each loop, but each needle had its own thread, and the rows of loops were vertical. Threads looped across from one vertical row to another, locking them together so the fabric did not unravel. Patterns of holes were created by leaving vertical rows unconnected at certain points according to the design.

The early stocking frames and warp frame machines were powered by hand or foot levers or treadles. Most were operated in the homes as a cottage industry.

Warp frame knitting, with vertical rows of loops. Threads cross to adjacent rows to make a fabric that does not unravel.

Handkerchief of machine-knit lace.

Twisting and Weaving Machines

Early in the 1800s, machines were developed that made net by twisting threads rather than by looping them. In 1808, John Heathcoat of Nottingham, England, patented the Bobbin Net (bobbinet) machine that duplicated the hexagonal mesh called *fond simple* made with bobbins. In this mesh, threads on four sides of hexagons are twisted twice, and on two sides the threads are crossed. As in bobbin lace, the moving threads traversed diagonally from one side to the other, rather than horizontally back and forth as on the warp frame or in regular weaving. The early machines were about eighteen inches wide and worked by turning a handle or by foot treadle. In 1816 Heathcoat built a large water wheel to drive larger machines, and he set up a steam powered plant in Paris two years later.

Wider pieces of net could be made on the bobbinet machine than could be made by hand. The lower price of the machine-made net made it practical to use the net to make new types of lace by embroidery and appliqué. Thousands of workers added sprigs of flowers and similar designs, copying the handmade laces that were popular at the time. Bobbinet was also used as a background for motifs of handmade bobbin lace (especially Honiton) and needle lace.

The Pusher machine, patented in 1812, was named for the long metal rods that pushed bobbins between warp threads. This modification of the bobbinet machine could make close reproductions of the whole stitch and the half stitch of bobbin lace. By the mid-1800s excellent reproductions of Chantilly laces with their large floral patterns were being made. Pusher laces were especially popular in the 1850s and 1860s when crinolines (hoop skirts) were in fashion. However, production by Pusher machines nearly ceased in the 1870s when changes in fashion caused a slump in the demand for these laces.

In 1813 the Levers machine was patented by John Levers of Nottingham. (Both his name and the name of the machine are also spelled Leavers.) The primary difference between this machine and Heathcoat's bobbinet machine was that Levers disc bobbins were thinner—there could be thirty bobbins to the inch—and only one row of bobbins was needed rather than two. The bobbins of the Levers machine consist of two very thin metal discs several inches in diameter joined in the center. The bobbins are mounted in thin carriages. The carriages run in grooves, moving forward and backward between the vertical warp threads, which move right or left for varying distances according to the pattern. Levers machines originally made a traversed net like bobbinet. Later modifications resulted in a "straight down" net (that is, the threads did not traverse diagonally). In 1828 Levers machines were adapted to steam power. Levers became the most versatile of the lace machines; they were capable of making an almost unlimited number of different patterns.

Machine-made lace resembling bobbin lace.

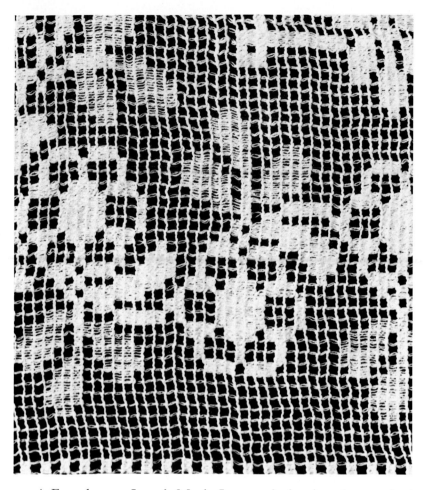

Curtain of machine-made lace resembling net darning.

A Frenchman, Joseph-Marie Jacquard, developed a punched card mechanism for looms to control patterns in woven fabric in 1801. Rods going through holes in a card determined the position of the warp threads in each row of weaving. The cards extended across the width of the patterned weaving and were linked with steel rods. As each row of weaving was completed the next card moved into place. The number of cards needed depended on the complexity of the pattern. The Jacquard technique for selective control of patterning threads was applied to warp frame, Pusher, and Levers machines around 1840.

The Lace Curtain machine was originated by John Livesay in 1846 at Nottingham. It is basically similar to the Levers, producing a straight down net. Each bobbin thread twists alternately with two warp threads, producing the characteristic square mesh. Shaded effects in the clothwork patterns result from varying the closeness of the horizontal connecting threads, taking them across more than one space and so overlapping, or introducing extra warp threads, usually heavier.

In 1846 the first practical sewing machine was patented in America by Elias Howe. Isaac Singer patented an improved model in 1851. Sewing machines made it possible for clothing to be ready-made at relatively low cost and for women to sew their own clothing more easily and quickly, thereby stimulating the demand for inexpensive lace.

In the latter part of the nineteenth century, machine reproductions of handmade laces were so exact that it is extremely difficult to tell some of the machine-made and handmade laces apart. As the sophistication of the machines increased, the quality of handmade lace decreased, because the workers tried to simplify their patterns and left out time-consuming details to speed production in a losing effort to stay competitive with the machines.

The Barmen machine was developed in the early 1900s in the Barmen area of Germany near the border of the Netherlands. It derived from braidmaking machines. The Barmen is circular in form, so it is also known as the circular braiding machine. It resembles a maypole, with large bobbins around the circumference and the threads converging toward a central tube. The movement of the bobbins, controlled by Jacquard apparatus, is equivalent to the twists and crosses of bobbin lace. Beaters rise after each movement of the bobbins to compact the lace and move it up the tube. The Barmen makes a cylinder of lace. A lacer or draw thread is worked into the lace so the cylinder can be opened out, forming a strip about eight inches wide. As many as four narrow widths can be made at the same time, joined by lacers to form a cylinder.

Today, steam and electricity power huge machines. The Jacquard technique automatically repeats a pattern throughout the length of the pieces of lace. Simple designs require only a dozen or so Jacquard cards, but as many as five thousand might be needed to produce large flowered patterns. Computer programs based on the Jacquard principles are in general use.

Across the width of the machine many lengths of edgings, insertions, or galloons are made at one time. These narrow widths are connected by lacer threads or narrow strips of net so the entire web can be taken off the machine in one piece to be mended, washed, bleached or dyed, stretched and stiffened before the individual strips are separated. Lacer threads are withdrawn or dissolved. Net connectors are cut, leaving slightly ragged edges.

An estimated 90 percent of the machine-made lace produced in the nineteenth century was made on Levers machines, but because they are ponderous, slow, and costly to operate, other types of machines have become more common. Synthetic fibers are well suited to machines based on the old warp frame machines. These Raschel machines produce nets, lace fabrics, and narrow edgings and insertions, as well as underwear and lightweight curtain material. Patterning is done by varying the interlocking of the vertical rows of loops and by incorporating other threads in the loops on the front surface. There are between 14 and 24 needles per inch across the 75- to 130-inch width of a Raschel machine. It can "knit" over 2,000 square inches per minute.

American manufacturers, such as the Quaker Lace Company of Philadelphia, began to provide serious competition to the Nottingham lace curtain industry in the early twentieth century.

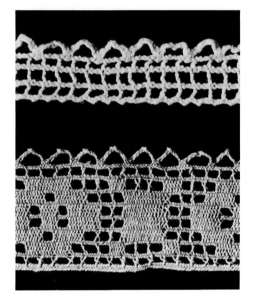

Above: Machine-made braided lace resembling crochet mesh and filet crochet.

Below: Machine-made lace resembling net darning.

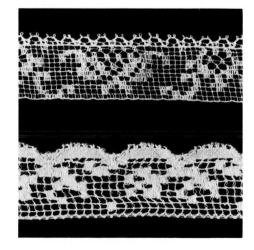

Later, as houses and windows became smaller, and tastes turned to simpler "modern" styles, lace curtains fell out of favor, but they again became popular with the wave of nostalgia beginning in the 1960s. The lace made on lace curtain machines can be recognized by its square mesh, zigzag fillings, shaded patterning, and strong parallel lines. The lace curtain machine makes large panels, primarily for curtains and tablecloths, but it also makes smaller articles such as table mats and a range of patterned and plain nets.

Levers machines can produce laces similar to those made on the lace curtain machine, but on a smaller scale. Raschel machines also make large panels, using synthetic fibers. The threads in Raschel laces are looped rather than twisted and the fabric is not reversible.

The Barmen accurately reproduces geometric patterns of bobbin lace, especially torchon, Cluny, and "val." Some edgings and insertions have the general appearance of filet crochet, but the threads are braided, not looped.

In the nineteenth century, the emphasis in machine-made lace was to reproduce handmade lace as closely as possible. At the close of the Victorian era, the importance of a handmade appearance declined, and the emphasis in machine-made lace shifted to designs more in keeping with a machine-oriented world.

Machine Embroidery

Several machines that made chain stitches similar to those made in tambour embroidery were developed in the early 1800s. The most successful one was patented in 1863 by a French engineer named Bonnaz. Its use became a cottage industry, especially in Switzerland. Stoles, collars, and shawls with Bonnaz chain stitching were made in large quantities. The Bonnaz machine was also used to appliqué muslin to net. Spachtel cutwork was made commercially with chain stitch sewing machines.

The so-called handmachine for embroidery was invented in Switzerland in 1828 by Josue Heilmann. This machine had many needles, all sewing replications of one pattern as they made the same stitch at the same time across the width of the fabric held rigidly in a frame. Two rows of pincers took the place of fingers holding the needles, which were pointed at each end with the eye in the middle. The first machine had twenty needles; later machines had over three hundred.

The handmachine operator moved the tracer of a pantograph from one stitch position to the next on an enlarged diagram of the pattern. As the jointed pantograph lever attached to the tracer and the frame holding the fabric moved, the frame moved. When the frame reached the correct position for the stitch, the operator manipulated the foot pedals that caused the row of pincers holding the needles to move forward so the needles pierced the fabric. These needle tips were then gripped by the other set of pincers, which pulled the needles through the fabric as the first set released their hold. The operator then moved the tracer to the next stitch position. These steps were repeated until the fabric in the frame had all been embroidered.

Satin stitch, outline stitch, and overcasting done by this machine cannot be distinguished from hand embroidery, except that the thread moves from one part of the design to another at exactly the same point in each repeat, and there are the same number of stitches in any given section of each repeat, which is rarely the case with hand embroidery. The machine does not make knot stitches. By 1860 hand machines had been adapted to work delicate filling stitches in holes that had been cut by mechanical borers.

The embroidery done by handmachines on lawn or muslin closely resembled handmade eyelet and Ayrshire work. Appliqué and embroidery on net resembled Carrickmacross and Limmerick needle-run lace except that the stitches did not follow the meshes of the net as precisely as in work done by hand.

By the early 1900s, the bigger, faster Schiffli machines dominated the machine embroidery industry. The Schiffli machine was invented in 1863 by Isaac Groebli. It uses continuous threads and hundreds of needles and boat-shaped bobbins. (*Shiffli* is German for "little boat.") The machines make a lock stitch with two threads, like the zigzag stitch of the home sewing machine. The needles have only one point. They are moved back and forth, piercing the fabric and interlocking the needle threads with the bobbin threads. The fabric is held taut in a frame twenty or more yards long. The frame is moved by the pantograph into the correct position for each stitch. The Jacquard attachment for the Schiffli was perfected around 1900.

The lock stitch is the only stitch that Schiffli machines make, but by varying the length, spacing, and tension of the stitches and by using different thicknesses of threads, laces that look as though they had been made by nearly all lacemaking techniques have been produced. Only the patterns and general appearances are duplicated, however. Careful examination with magnification will show that the stitches characterizing handmade laces are not present, and the results have been achieved with variations of the lock stitch.

Schiffli machines produce two types of lace:

1. Embroidery on a fabric that is part of the finished lace—eyelet edgings and insertions, for example, or machine-embroidered net. When the embroidery is worked on net, the net must be supported in the frame with a specially prepared backing fabric. When the embroidery is completed, a hot iron or oven, or a singeing flame chars the backing fabric so it can be brushed away. In some designs thinner thread is used to fill in leaves, petals, etc. The embroidery bears no particular relation to the net itself—threads do not go in and out of the net as in hand work.

Machine-embroidered eyelet "beading." The slits are made to thread ribon through for added decorative effect.

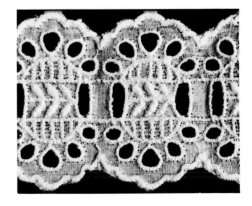

A small mat with machine-embroidered eyelet designs.

2. Embroidery on a backing, which will be removed so only the embroidery stitches remain. Experiments with this process began in 1879, based on the chemical differences between animal fibers such as wool and silk, which are protein based, and plant fibers such as cotton and linen, which are cellulose. The stitching was done with cotton thread on a background of silk or wool, which was then dissolved with a suitable corrosive, such as chlorine or caustic soda. Backings commonly used now are acetate rayon, which dissolves in acetone, or cotton fabric pretreated with acid so it will disintegrate in hot air or in hot water. These laces are called *chemical* or *burned laces*. This method has been used to imitate many types of lace. Although the designs may closely duplicate needle lace, crochet, or tatting, the stitches are zigzag lock stitches. Chemical lace can usually be identified by the scrambled look of the threads when studied under magnification, and by the fuzzy appearance of the threads at the edges of solid areas.

Switzerland, Austria, and Germany were the centers of the machine embroidered lace industry until World War I, when many firms closed. Machine embroidery in America started as a cottage industry in New Jersey in 1903, with workers purchasing Schiffli machines on the installment plan. New Jersey now ranks first in world production of machine embroidered fabric. Ninety percent of the embroidery machines in the United States now operate in an area along the Hudson River above Jersey City.

Left: A collar of "chemical" lace, resembling needle lace.

Below: Machine embroidery on fabric, background removed ("chemical" lace), resembling needle lace.

Machine embroidery on net. Heavier
thread outlines the design areas and fills
the circles; finer thread adds shading to the
petals and large leaf shapes.

Preservation and Use

Laces have a unique and particular charm. They are pure decoration, beautiful expressions of fiber art developed to enhance wearing apparel or the home. If the preservation of these items for future generations is most important to you, you will want to record all you know about them, then clean and store them so that they will last for others to enjoy. Be sure to share your interest in these items with other family members so they are aware that the laces are treasures to be preserved.

If you decide to surround yourself with the beauty of lace, and enjoy its visual quality, you will want to clean and mount some of your treasures for display.

If you wish to use lacy items as they were made to be used or to use them in another context, you will want to clean, restore, and possibly remake them into usable items for today.

If you believe that some of your items may be very old and have great historical or personal value, it is best to consult an expert who will be able to help you identify and date the items and suggest cleaning and storage methods.

Recording

Pieces of lace we find in trunks and attics, saved by families because of their beauty and sentimental worth, are a lovely tangible link with our roots. Search out as much information about items that belonged to your family as you can. Talk with an older family member. Take lots of notes—usually going through the lace pieces will jog all sorts of memories about family history. You may discover that Great-aunt Jane made many filet crochet doilies that she gave to family members, and Uncle Joe brought back lovely lace gloves and hankies when he returned from France after World War I. Going through family photographs may help you identify some pieces of lace. You may find a picture of a collar that is in your collection, worn for that important portrait. Promptly write down everything you discover before the memory fades and the information is lost. These records will make fascinating reading for family members. Include information about the people who owned or made the lace—even a family tree. Include photographs and dates and events, and how and where the lacemakers learned their skills.

A Hardanger edging trims the scarf on a dressing table.

Record what you know about the other pieces of lace in your collection, too—kind of lace, probable use (doily, collar, etc.), where you obtained it or who gave it to you, price if you bought it, the date you obtained it, and a description. Leave enough space so you can add more information if you find it, such as the probable date the item was made, or where the directions for that pattern were printed.

If you can include in your record book photocopies or sketches of the lace pieces in your collection, they will help future generations identify the pieces.

Labeling

Make identifying labels on strips of white cloth or interfacing, using a laundry marker pen or a typewriter, and carefully baste or tie the labels to the items. Develop an identification key to connect the label with the more detailed account and description in the record book. For example, the record book might list items by type of lace in the chronological order you acquired them. The identification label might say only "Crochet 12, 6/85," or it could include type of article, former owner, and other identifying characteristics. Have some information attached to the items themselves in case the record book is lost.

Do not pin labels to the items—pins may snag delicate fabrics and may rust or corrode. Don't use adhesive labels—they leave a sticky residue on fabrics.

Stabilizing

After you have recorded and labeled your lace, look carefully at each item and decide what must be done next. In some rare instances items may have been carefully and properly stored. However, most family accumulations of lace have been stored in attics and basements in dusty out of the way places in drafty old houses. These storage places have probably the worst possible climate for preserving old textiles. When we acquire pieces of lace, they are often stained, yellowed, or grayed, weakened by effects of poor storage conditions, or damaged by insects or rodents. Logically, the first step is to stop ongoing damage. The next step is to clean the items and then to store them in such a way that future damage will be minimized.

When you are handling lace, do not wear rings or bracelets with prongs or points that might catch the threads of the lace. Snagging a thread can result in a major repair job.

To spare disappointment and extra effort, a careful examination of each piece of lace to discover fiber damage is important. If the lace has been damaged, it should be stabilized to prevent further tearing or unraveling before other steps are taken. The nature of some lacemaking techniques, especially looping (crochet and knitting), makes the saying "a stitch in time saves nine" very true. If left untended, these pieces of lace can unravel, and the damage will travel rapidly through the piece. Catch the loose and broken threads to stop more unraveling. For temporary stabilizing, use fine thread in a contrasting color and carefully catch each loop or thread end around the damaged area. This colored thread will remind you that repair work is needed, and will be removed later when the repairs are made. A soft support fabric should be basted under torn or worn areas so they won't tear further when the lace is handled.

Cleaning

In most cases, a careful cleaning will next be in order. There are almost as many ideas, theories, and methods of cleaning lace as there are collectors. Listed are some ideas from which you may choose the one that best suits each individual item in your collection, depending upon what you have decided to do with it. Do you want to store some of your lace pieces for future generations? Do you wish to mount some as works of art to display in your home? Do you want to use some lace pieces as they were made to be used—as tablecloths, doilies, or collars and cuffs? Have you decided to remodel or remake some items for today's clothing or interior design? Your plans for each item will determine your next steps.

If you decide to use a lace item to decorate clothing or household linens, clean it as you plan to clean the decorated article. To preserve lace for future generations, follow the cleaning procedures suggested by fabric preservationists.

When deciding how to clean and store your lace, be aware of conditions and factors that can be harmful to fibers:

- *Extreme temperature changes* (found in many attics, garages, and basements) are harmful to fibers. Temperatures between 65 and 75 degrees F. are best.

- *Ultraviolet light* (in sunshine and in fluorescent light) deteriorates fibers rapidly.

- *Moisture* often causes damage from mildew and molds. Humidity between 45 and 55 percent is ideal. Excessive dryness makes fibers brittle, so a fabric should not be ironed before storage.

- *Acids* in wood, cardboard, and paper deteriorate fibers. Storage places for fabrics should be lined with acid-free materials.

- *Plastic bags* should not be used for long-time storage of fabrics. Dry cleaner bags made of polyvinylchloride (PVC) give off gases that combine with moisture to form hydrochloric acid (a fabric eater). Polyurethane is a stable plastic, but moisture may condense inside the plastic and cause mildew to form. The static electricity of plastic bags attracts dust and grime. Moth crystals will dissolve plastic bags.

• *Bleaches* will destroy fibers if they remain in contact for any length of time.

• *Minerals* in water may cause rust stains to develop during longtime storage. As a safety precaution, use distilled (or demineralized) water, especially for the final rinses.

• *Creasing* (folding) will break fibers along the crease line. Where possible, store lace flat or rolled on tubes protected with acid-free paper or muslin. If folding is necessary, use loose folds softened with crushed acid-free paper or nylon net that has been washed. Items should occasionally be refolded in a different pattern to reduce the strain on the fibers.

• *Stiffeners* such as starch and sugar solutions were often used to shape doilies, baskets, and collars and cuffs. These stiffeners should be removed from lace before storage because the starch and sugar attract insects and rodents and will absorb moisture.

Each time you wash a piece of lace you may be surprised. Perhaps it will come out snowy white. Perhaps stains will refuse to come out no matter what you do, or the piece may fall apart. These are the risks, but doing nothing is also risky. Wet cleaning will restore cotton and linen to a neutral condition by removing acids picked up from paper and wood storage containers and from the atmosphere, resulting in longer life for your lace.

The steps listed below outline methods and materials often used by textile preservationists. After stabilizing damaged areas to prevent further deterioration, do the following steps in order, stopping when the desired results have been achieved:

Step 1. Remove loose dirt

Vacuum a piece of lace before going on to another cleaning process or putting the lace in storage. Vacuuming removes loose dirt, which would turn to mud when dampened, and also removes mold spores and insect eggs, which would cause damage in storage.

Vacuuming is the only cleaning process that should be used for any article that is fragile or of unknown fiber content. It is not necessary to distinguish between cotton and linen, because the same cleaning methods can be used on both these cellulose fibers. Animal fibers—silk and wool—are discussed on page 154.

Vacuum gently. Cover the nozzle of the vacuum cleaner with a nylon stocking or other soft porous fabric, held in place with a rubber band. Place nylon net or a fiberglass screen over the lace. Fiberglass can be purchased at hardware stores. Tape or cover all cut edges of the screen to avoid snagging the lace. Use the weakest suction setting. Vacuum across the lace horizontally, then vertically. Turn the lace over and vacuum the other side.

Step 2. Support

Support each item that is to be wet cleaned by basting it carefully to clean muslin or net, or by sandwiching it between two layers of fiberglass screening. Unless lace is carefully handled, the weight of the water absorbed by the fibers may damage the lace. Baste fragile items to a clean, bleach-free fabric. When basting the lace to the support fabric, stitch between the threads of the lace; do not pierce the fibers with the needle. Then lay the supported lace on a fiberglass screen to support it while it is being wet cleaned. Less fragile items can simply be laid on a fiberglass screen and covered with a second screen.

Step 3. Presoak

Immerse the supported lace in distilled water and soak for at least half an hour. The water should be lukewarm or at room temperature to avoid fabric stress. Lace may shrink in hot water. Lower the supported lace carefully into the water, avoiding strong pressure. Do not pour water directly on the lace or rub the fibers. Gently slosh the water through the lace occasionally. Distilled water should be used for this step because this presoak may clean the article sufficiently so that no further cleaning is necessary. If the article is clean but stained, go to Step 5. If it is clean and not stained, go to step 6.

Step 4. Washing

If the presoak does not clean the article as desired, soak it in a lukewarm detergent or soap solution. There are many opinions about what soaps or detergents to use for washing lace. The best rule to remember is that lace is fragile and caution should be exercised. Most authorities agree that if soap is used it should be one that does not contain perfumes, color brighteners, bleaches, fabric softeners, hand lotion, or coloring. Some examples of pure soaps are Ivory and Neutrogena (original formula, unscented). Soaps are easier on fibers than detergents are, but they are more difficult to rinse out completely and they may not clean as well. Thus many experts recommend using soapless detergents. Be sure the detergent is free of additives that can affect the fabric. An example of a non-ionic detergent, often used by museums, is Orvus. Some authorities recommend enzyme cleansers such as Biz and Axion. Most experts warn that wool soaps are not recommended for cleaning lace because they contain damaging additives.

When using a dry soap product such as Ivory Snow, dissolve about one-half cup in an equal amount of hot water to make a gel. Use about two tablespoons of the gel per quart of wash water or enough to make the water feel "silky." If using a bar soap such as Neutrogena, dissolve about one-eighth of a 3.5 ounce bar in a cup of water; use one ounce of this solution to a gallon of wash water.

Use an ounce of non-ionic detergent to a gallon of wash water. Follow package directions if using an enzyme cleanser.

Remember that the more soap or detergent is used, the more rinsing is needed.

Do not make suds. Skim off any suds or curds on the wash water before immersing the fabric and before lifting it out of the water so they will not be trapped in the fibers.

Soak the lace in the soap or detergent solution for an hour, gently sloshing the wash water through the lace occasionally. Rinse. If the article still appears dirty, repeat the washing.

Rinse thoroughly, using distilled water for at least the last several rinses. Detergent-soaked lace should be rinsed a minimum of five times; soap-soaked items should be rinsed more times. Using a fiberglass support screen protects wet fibers but retards the rinsing, so more rinses are needed than in ordinary laundering.

Step 5. Stain removal

Before you try any stain removal, you need to decide whether you would rather have your article whole with stains, or whiter but damaged, because these are realistic options. Stains are color changes within the fibers. Some will come out quite readily, but others will not respond to any treatment, and trying to remove them will only weaken or destroy the fibers.

Some stains will diminish or disappear if the fabric is soaked in water for several days. You may wish to try this before using a more drastic process to remove stains. If the lace remains yellowed or stained, bleaching may be helpful. There are many opinions as to how stains should be treated. Use whichever method you feel comfortable with and achieves your desired results, starting with the gentlest process and progressing to more rigorous methods only if necessary. Some authorities say the enzyme bleaches such as Biz and Axion are best (follow package directions; do not use on wool or silk). Some authorities recommend using hydrogen peroxide: mix 5/7 ounce of 30 percent hydrogen peroxide in one quart of distilled water. Soak the lace in this solution no longer than five minutes, then wrap the piece in clear plastic and leave until the desired whiteness is observed—but do not leave wrapped longer than three hours. Rinse thoroughly in distilled water. Most fabric preservationists agree that chlorine bleach is too harsh to be used on lace. They all agree that whatever bleach is used, very thorough rinsing is needed to remove all bleach residue.

Some people like to use sunshine to whiten cotton and linen. Our mothers had great success with lemon juice, salt, and a clear sunny day for removing stains on table linens. (Make a paste of salt and lemon juice; apply to the stained area and place the fabric in the sun for half an hour or so.) Lemon juice and sunshine will remove some stains. Sunlight alone is a time-honored bleach. We do not know how many items did not get passed on to the present generation because of ultraviolet deterioration during sun bleaching, but a little common sense and care should get the desired results without serious problems. It is over a period of time in constant sunlight that fibers degrade.

Food and beverage stains are commonly found on old lace pieces, especially on tablecloths, table runners, and doilies. The tea, coffee, wine, and fruit stains that did not come out with ordinary washing methods may respond to one of the following treatments:

1. Soak for fifteen minutes in a solution of one quart of warm distilled water and one-half teaspoon liquid hand dishwashing detergent and one tablespoon white vinegar. Rinse thoroughly.

2. Sponge the stain with denatured alcohol. Wash and rinse thoroughly.

3. Soak in a solution of one tablespoon Borax in one cup of distilled water. Rinse thoroughly.

Oil-based stains (makeup, cream, gravy, grease, wax) should first be sponged with a dry cleaning solvent. Apply the solvent with a cotton swab, after placing clean absorbent cloth under the lace. Work from the edges of the spot toward the center to keep the stain from spreading or leaving a ring. If the stain persists, dry completely, then sponge with water. Next, mix one teaspoon of glycerin, one teaspoon of hand dishwashing detergent, two tablespoons of water, and a few drops of ammonia. Wet the stain with this mixture and blot with absorbent material. Continue wetting and blotting until no more color from the stain comes out. Rinse thoroughly.

Brown spots on linens and lace often have resulted from acid in cardboard and wood containers. Where these spots, scorch stains, and mildew are present, the fibers are damaged and weakened. Any attempt at stain removal may further damage the fibers. Gentle hydrogen peroxide bleaching may whiten the browned fibers, but proceed very cautiously.

Oxalic acid (one tablespoon oxalic acid crystals in one cup warm distilled water) will remove some rust stains, but may also remove the fibers. Commercial preparations are available for removing rust stains, but don't use them or oxalic acid on delicate or valuable lace.

Some items may disintegrate entirely even if washed very gently. If this happens, console yourself with the fact that years of neglect, poor storage conditions, improper cleaning, exposure to ultraviolet light, or a combination of these factors caused the damage, not the final washing.

Step 6. Drying

After the last rinse, lay the article flat on an undyed, chlorine-free cloth towel and allow to dry at room temperature. (Remember that paper towels may contain harmful acids.) If the item was basted to a support, leave it on the support to dry; it will usually dry smooth without wrinkles. Heat from an iron is harmful to fibers, so ironing should be avoided. If the lace is not basted to a support, smooth it while still wet onto a sheet of glass, plastic laminate, or enameled surface and allow to dry. The top of the washer or dryer or a kitchen counter works well for this. Smooth gently. Work the lace into shape with the thumb and finger. This will give the lace an ironed look. Some large items may be handled better by drying first, then rewetting and smoothing onto the glass surface, one section at a time.

If you feel that ironing is necessary, use a cool iron and iron from the back. Take care not to catch the lace on the sharp tip of the iron. It is best to use a press cloth when ironing lace, because the rough texture of the lace may scrape discoloration from the iron.

Some laces need to be pinned out to shape, either while damp or dampened after pinning. Use a sheet of foam insulation board or craft styrofoam, covered with plastic or wax paper. The shape of the doily, collar, medallion, etc., can be drawn on paper which is put under the plastic or wax paper. Gently arrange the lace so it is the correct size and shape and pin the points, picots, petals, etc., in their proper positions, using rustproof pins. Allow to dry at room temperature.

If a piece of lace needs to be stretched to fit a certain shape — the frame of a fan, for example — you may need to do the stretching in two or more steps to minimize the chances of thread breakage. Center the lace on the pattern on the pinning board and pin the edges as close to the outline as the lace will comfortably fit. Dampen the lace and let it dry. Then gently stretch the lace so it can be pinned a little closer to the outline. Dampen and let dry. Repeat as needed.

Cleaning Silk and Wool

Silk is an animal fiber composed of the insoluble protein fibroin, unwound from the cocoons of silkworms. The continuous filament from a single cocoon may be more than a mile long. Varying numbers of these filaments are used together to make different weights of thread. Shorter lengths of filament from damaged cocoons are spun together. Silk is prized for its luster and softness, and for its lightness and strength.

Silk is the most sensitive of all natural fibers to ultraviolet light. The fibers gradually weaken and eventually disintegrate. Moisture and sunlight accelerate the decomposition. In the nineteenth and early twentieth centuries, silk was treated with metal salts to add weight so the silk fabric would drape well. These salts make weighted silk brittle and very sensitive to handling and sunlight.

Wool is animal hair made of the protein keratin. Most wool comes from domestic sheep, but goat, llama, and alpaca wools are also used. Wool fibers are covered with tiny scales that help the fibers cling together in spinning, but make the threads too rough for many forms of lacemaking. Wool yarn is commonly used for knitting and crocheting shawls, scarfs, sweaters, and other articles of clothing. The scales on the fibers tend to hook together when agitated during washing, resulting in felting and shrinkage. Wool slowly deteriorates in sunlight and prolonged exposure to dry heat.

Silk and wool can be washed, but handle them very gently. Hydrogen peroxide is the recommended bleach for silks.

Animal fibers may be dry cleaned rather than washed, but only if it seems absolutely necessary. Dry cleaning is hard on fibers because the items being cleaned are tumbled in vats of harsh chemicals. Choose a dry cleaner who will give your items special care. Ask that they be the first items cleaned in a new batch of cleaning solvent, or that they be hand cleaned. Delicate items should be basted between layers of nylon tulle to support them while they are being dry cleaned.

Repairing and Restoring

For very old and precious pieces of lace it is wise to consult an expert for advice. If a piece has historic value, antiques dealers and collectors feel that altering it (even mending) reduces its value. This reservation does not apply to most of the pieces of lace that we are likely to find in trunks and attics.

Lace is often stronger than the cloth to which it was attached, so a piece of lace may have been reused several times before it came to you. If the cloth is worn but the lace still usable, replacing the cloth will give the item a new life. If the lace itself is tattered and torn, mending is a possibility. If the nature of the damage is such that the fibers can be replaced and reworked, you can make repairs that will be "as good as new." The secret to good repair is in finding thread that matches the original in fiber content, size, and color. Sometimes age has changed the color, often unevenly, and you may need to "antique" the thread to achieve a match. Dye test pieces, drying them completely to assure that they are the right color. In some cases you may have better results starting with a darker shade and bleaching to achieve a color match.

Make up samples to develop your skill and match the style, duplicating the techniques used to make the original lace piece. Then you are ready to remake the damaged portion, carefully securing all broken fibers.

In some cases you may wish merely to reinforce the damaged area with an almost invisible material. Pure silk illusion net is a good choice for making this type of repair. Nylon net is too stiff and crisp and could cause damage to soft old fibers. Use a fine silk or cotton thread and attach the lace to the net patch with tiny stitches that loop around the lace fibers but do not pierce them. It may help to work on a dark surface such as black velveteen or suede so you can see the fine net. The velveteen surface will also help hold the lace and net in place as you work.

If the damaged areas are large and your skills do not include that particular lacemaking technique, you might consider patchwork for repair. You could fill in or cover damaged or missing areas using other pieces of lace. This is most effective if motifs are cut out and inserted, repeating the design elements and using creative needlework to camouflage the patching. If a symmetrical design is involved, repeat the motif addition to balance the design even where the lace is not damaged. You might add some embroidered leaves or stems to cover the seamlines and to balance the design. Be sure to catch all the fiber ends and loops that are loose, especially with knit or crocheted lace, so the work does not continue to unravel.

Storing Lace

With your laces cleaned and refreshed, you need to decide how to store them. There are certain precautions you should take to ensure long life for your treasured pieces of lace. Keep in mind the causes of fiber damage listed on page 149 and try to avoid them.

Ordinary paper, cardboard, and wood have harmful acids that stain or destroy many fibers. If you want to store your lace in cardboard boxes or wooden chests, first line the storage area with an acid-free material. Old white cotton pillowcases or sheets that have no bleach residue are excellent for lining the storage area or for wrapping the lace. Acid-free tissue paper can be purchased and used to line the storage containers and also to wrap the items or pad folded areas. (Check with your local museum or university to find a source for acid-free paper and other conservation supplies.) Acid-free paper and fabric liners gradually take up acid from wood and cardboard containers and transfer it to the stored articles with which they are in contact, so the paper should be replaced and the fabric liners should be laundered periodically.

Cedar chests have long been considered to be a perfect place to

Two pairs of delicate lace gloves, one knitted and the other netted, are shown here on a steamer trunk.

store treasured heirlooms. They do a fairly good job of discouraging moths from attacking woolens, but the acids in the cedar wood will yellow cottons and linens and disintegrate silk. A cedar chest should be lined or the articles should be wrapped in nonacid material to prevent contact with the wood, and the chest should be vented or aired occasionally to remove the harmful buildup of gases.

Old trunks and chests made of wood were often lined in calico print wallpaper using casien or starch glues. This environment can result in a bad case of yellow stains, and it attracts chewing insects. Carefully lining these containers and providing ventilation will create tolerable storage conditions.

Aluminum foil can be used to line surfaces where lace is stored. The lining can be stapled or pinned in place to ensure that the wood or cardboard does not make contact with the lace. Be careful that all staples or pins used are placed so they will not snag the lace, and that they are nonrusting.

Wood and sturdy cardboard containers can be sealed by painting or coating with a polyurethane finish.

Plastic bags should not be used for long-time storage of lace. They give off harmful gases and condense any moisture trapped inside the bag. The moisture then combines with the gas to make hydrochloric acid, which destroys fibers. Moisture can also result in mildew formation. Another negative aspect of plastic bags is their static charge that attracts dust and grime, soiling the lace.

Where possible, store lace items flat in lined containers, with acid-free material layered between the items. To avoid creases that can break the fibers, the lace can be rolled on cardboard tubes (covered or sealed) or on rolls of acid-free paper. For larger items, fold loosely and pad the folds with rolls of acid-free material. Pack the lace loosely to avoid crushing or creasing. Do not stack heavy items on top of other items.

Traditionally we have stored not-often-used treasures in out of the way places such as attics and basements. These parts of our homes are usually neither heated nor air-conditioned, and so are prone to wide extremes of temperature and humidity. Ideally, fabrics should be kept in a temperature range that is comfortable for people and at a relative humidity of 50 percent or lower. In today's homes a good storage location would be a closet in a room that is kept comfortable for living in.

Storage arrangements that protect articles from dust, insects, rodents, and similar hazards will usually also protect them from ultraviolet light, but check to see that exposure to light is minimized.

Be sure to take your stored items down off the shelf or out of the boxes occasionally so that you can air them out, refold on new lines, replace the acid-free materials protecting them, and admire the beauty of your lace. If treated with care and respect, lace will last to give pleasure to future generations.

Displaying Lace

Some of the lace you own may be too beautiful to be hidden away in a closet and only enjoyed at air-out time. There are many ways you can display your lace pieces. A lovely piece of lace mounted against a dark background to highlight the intricate pattern can rival a painting as an exciting work of art.

When mounting, framing, and hanging lace items, keep in mind the list of causes of fiber damage. Any wood, paper, or cardboard used should be acid-free or covered or sealed to prevent fabric contact. Check with a reliable picture framer and your local museum for information about mounting precious fabrics. Museum board can be purchased for mounting the lace, or the mounting board can be covered with acid-free material or sealed with an inert sealant such as polyurethane.

A dark colored background will display white or off-white lace patterns most successfully. Choose a fabric with no harmful additives or finishes, or one that can be washed clean of all harmful chemicals. Cotton velveteen is an excellent choice for backing lace and comes in a wide variety of colors.

Attach the lace to the mounting material carefully by hand, using cotton or silk thread. Avoid polyester and nylon threads as they tend to cut fragile fibers. Avoid splitting the lace threads; instead, place the needle between the threads of the lace. Secure well, but do not pull the stitches tight.

If you choose to use glass to keep dust off your mounted lace, make sure the glass will not touch the lace. Condensation on the glass surface may be transferred to the fibers, causing mold to grow. Leave space enough (one-quarter inch minimum) to allow the lace to expand and breathe. The back of the picture should be left unsealed but covered with a breathable dust catcher. A prewashed flannel stapled to the back of the frame will filter dust out. This flannel backing should be changed or washed occasionally to keep the lace clean. Any backing used should breathe

Needle lace mat (detail shown on page 115).

to prevent a buildup of harmful moisture and chemicals.

Large lace items such as tablecloths and bedspreads can be hung without a frame. Line the lace with a compatible material that will support and take the weight off the lace. Sew the lace onto the backing by hand, using cotton or silk thread and taking care not to split the fibers. Sew a pocket onto the backing along the top to hold a rigid bar. This bar will support the hanging evenly and avoid stress points. All fabric wall hangings need to rest occasionally. When you take the hanging down, vacuum it carefully to remove dust, fold it loosely with the creases padded or roll it on a tube, and store it in a dark place. If possible, rotate the hanging so it hangs from a different side the next time it is displayed.

A vase of lace medallion flowers sits on a handkerchief tablecloth beside a window curtain of embroidered net in this appliqué picture made by Shirley Nilsson.

An occasional vacuuming will prolong the life of fabrics not protected by glass. Use a soft brush that has been covered with a nylon stocking and use low suction.

When you choose a location to hang your lace, remember the list of harmful conditions. Avoid direct sunlight and strong reflected light. Incandescent light is less damaging than fluorescent. Heating units, if too close, can cause temperature extremes and severe drying of the fibers. Kitchens, laundry rooms, and bathrooms usually have high humidity levels that can be harmful to the fibers. To reduce fading and degradation problems, mount several pieces of similar size and style and rotate their display,

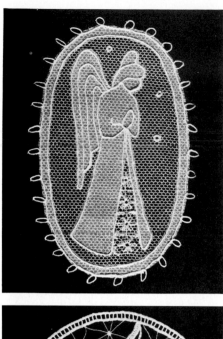

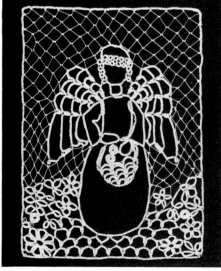

Kathleen Warnick collects angels and makes new ones to practice lacemaking techniques. Her Carrickmacross, needle lace, and tatting angels are mounted as small pictures.

keeping each one out for only a short period of time. This also provides an opportunity to enjoy a changing view of different pieces.

Lace can be displayed in ways other than framing or hanging. Glass-topped coffee and end tables are sometimes constructed to display flat items. Glass-topped serving trays effectively display lace doilies. Use the same precautions in mounting the items as you would in framing them. A china cabinet or breakfront lined with dark velvet makes a lovely display case for lace pieces, and lace makes a beautiful background for china, silver, and crystal.

There are some lace items that would lend themselves very well to a three-dimensional or sculptural display. Items such as collars, handbags, baskets, fans, gloves, and hats are exquisite displayed on a tabletop, perhaps under a glass dome. Lace items can be incorporated into a wall grouping that includes a variety of memorabilia such as an old photograph, handkerchief, pair of glasses, nostalgic valentine, and grandpa's watch and chain. A shadow box or cabinet can display a collection of lace and other objects. If you have samples of lace your grandmother made, you may also have the tools she used to make them. Display a handkerchief edged in tatting with her shuttle. An eyelet doily could be displayed with an ivory stiletto, embroidery scissors, thimble, and needle case. Round out the display with a photograph of the creative lacemaker. Mount an exquisite lace collar in a shadow box frame and use it as the background for a small fashion doll dressed in a costume of the period.

Collecting with a Focus

Our interest in lace began because we had some family attic collections. As we acquired more pieces, we realized that we wanted to categorize them by the technique used in making them. We discovered more information about lace, and our collections grew. We soon found that although it is nice to own some interesting pieces of lace, it is much more rewarding to collect with a definite focus. One can, of course, have more than one focus. Here are ideas of ways to group lace collections:

Examples of all the different lacemaking techniques you can find (then keep looking for better examples)

Different articles made with one technique

One type of item (such as collars) made using different techniques

General design subjects such as animals, flowers, or mythical characters, or specific subjects such as horses, roses, or unicorns

Tools used in lacemaking, such as tatting shuttles or lace bobbins

When friends and relatives know the focus of your collection, they will soon be adding to it.

Using Lace

Pieces of lace are beautiful examples of exquisite craftsmanship, decorative elements made to be used for enhancing clothing or homes. Many old pieces of lace can be used today just as they were intended to be used when they were lovingly crafted many years ago.

Old laces which are of historic or sentimental value should be carefully preserved for future generations. (Do not underestimate how quickly the generations pass. When you give your granddaughter a piece of lace your grandmother owned, you are giving her something which was her great-great grandmother's.) You should also preserve laces which are outstanding examples of design and/or craftsmanship, or which were made in unusual techniques.

Other old laces might just as well be put to use today so their beauty can be enjoyed, either in the ways they were made to be used or in new ways. It is better to use lacy articles which are not special enough to be given first-rate storage treatment, than to relegate them to dusty attics or damp basements where they will deteriorate past any usefulness.

Because lacemaking takes time, skill, and patience, and because lace is beautiful, pieces of lace have been treasured. When a lace-trimmed garment or household linen wore out, the lace was usually removed before the item was discarded. These pieces of lace were then used again as decoration, sometimes alone and sometimes in combination with other lace pieces.

In the following section are suggestions of ways to use old laces, but the suggestions are equally applicable to machine-made and new handmade laces.

Lace for Clothing

Lace collars are beautiful fashion statements. An ordinary outfit can become something special with the addition of a piece of intricate openwork at the neckline. A century ago, lace collars were designed and worn to protect non-washable silk and woolen clothing from body oils and make-up. They also protected tender skin from the scratchiness of harsh woolen fabrics. The collars were attached with hand stitching or small snap fasteners so they could be easily removed for cleaning. Now the emphasis has

This tunic was fashioned from an old machine-made lace tablecloth. The pattern pieces were placed so the center design of the tablecloth surrounds the neck and the scalloped edge forms the bottom hem.

changed, and today the often heard question is "How can I protect my antique lace collar from excessive soil and wear?"

Some lace collars can be worn on a blouse or dress with a plain high neckline, just as you would wear a beautiful necklace. A larger or longer collar might be worn under the collar of a dress, held in place with a few stitches or a jeweled pin. A collar can be sewed a short distance (one-quarter to one-half inch) below the neck edge of a collarless blouse, sweater, or dress, leaving a uniform strip of the garment at the neckline to emphasize the collar and to protect it from body oils.

The yoke of this blouse was originally the crocheted edging of a large doily.

Most old laces need to be treated much more gently than clothing made of modern fabrics, so old lace collars should be attached to garments in such a way that they can be easily removed when either the garment or the collar needs to be cleaned. Fine lace used to be sewed to a narrow strip of plainer lace, which in turn was sewed to a garment. This strip would be replaced when it wore out. The same principle still works—sew a strip of compatible fabric such as net, lace, ribbon, or bias tape along the neck edge of the collar to be either sewed to a garment or tucked inside the neckline.

When sewing a lace collar to a garment or an edging strip, take very small stitches around the threads of the lace, not piercing the fibers, and longer stitches on the inside of the garment so they can be easily found and safely clipped when the collar is to be removed from the garment.

Most laces made today can withstand ordinary laundry methods and can be cleaned with the garment. Some will need to be pressed back into shape, either with the fingers while damp, or very carefully with an iron and damp press cloth.

Lace pieces that were made for other purposes can be adapted to become fashion accents. For example, the lace edging on a pillowcase can be removed and re-used to dress up the neckline of a shirt or blouse.

Lace medallions or doilies can be appliquéd onto a padded

jacket or vest and then quilted to accent the design. Or a doily could be appliquéd onto a tote bag for a fashion accessory.

The wide lace edging on a doily with a fabric center at least seven inches in diameter can be made into an over-the-head collar or the yoke for a blouse or dress. Carefully rip out the sewing stitches that attached the lace to the fabric. If the lace was worked directly into the fabric, as was common with crocheting and netting, cut the fabric one-half inch from the lace and make a narrow rolled hem. Run a cord or ribbon around the inner edge so the opening can be adjusted to the desired size.

Five or six small doilies side by side or overlapped would make a different type of collar or yoke.

Doilies appliquéd on a white quilted jacket produce interesting textural effects. The lace on the shoulders is crocheted and in the center back is Battenberg.

Lace in Home Decorating

Many lace pieces such as tablecloths, curtains, bedspreads, dresser scarves, placemats, and doilies, were made to enhance the home. In contemporary use, tablecloths have moved from the dining room and are now also used for decorative accents in bedrooms and living rooms. A simple round end table might be covered with a colorful plain floor length cloth, then topped with a smaller round or square lace cloth.

If you have a high-backed chair with upholstered arms that seem to soil quickly, use antimacassars, whose original purpose was to protect backs and arms of upholstered furniture. These can also help hide faded and worn spots on your chairs or sofa. A side chair upholstered in a dark plain fabric can be given new importance by just adding a lacy antimacassar.

Doilies were designed primarily to protect the highly polished surfaces of mahogany, cherry, and walnut furniture popular in Victorian and Edwardian times. The finishes were vulnerable to scratching, moisture, and heat. Lace doilies allowed plants and scratchy objets d'art to be placed on the furniture without causing damage. Dark furniture surfaces today can effectively show off your lace doilies, which will enhance displays of flowers or china.

A lace doily can cover a "not so perfect" wood table top. Many lacy articles are not useful to us today in their original forms. Following are examples of how these lovely pieces might be used in new ways.

Doilies were made in a variety of shapes and sizes, created by every method of lacemaking. They probably constitute the bulk of the lace pieces made in the last century which have survived for our use and pleasure. Table runners, antimacassars and dresser scarves are also frequently found, and can be used in similar ways.

Most doilies are ideal shapes for pillows. Backed by colorful plain fabric to show off the intricate pattern, they make striking additions to bedrooms or living rooms. Or try white lace on white background (or beige-on-beige) to create subtle textural interest. Center a doily as a medallion on a larger pillow or make a pillow the same shape as a doily. Use several doilies on one pillow, side by side or overlapped to create special effects.

Doilies of waffle work and net darning were mounted on dark fabric to make these pillows.

Doilies can also be used as place mats. On a dark table top or colorful plain cloth, they make a lovely accent for fine china and crystal. They don't need to be all the same—set an interesting table with a variety of compatible designs. Two long dresser scarves crossed in the middle of a table form an elegant setting for four.

Small doilies can be used as flower shapes to make a large bouquet on a bed cover or quilt. Embroider stems or use narrow strips of lace or ribbon, add appliquéd fabric or lace leaves, and quilt in a lattice pattern.

An interesting quilt can be made by centering doilies in squares or oblongs of colored fabric and joining these blocks in a pleasing design. Odd-shaped doilies could be joined to make a romantic "crazy quilt" effect. A table runner could be the center motif, using doilies around it for another effect. Small round doilies could be used as centers for large "Dresden plate" quilt blocks. Appliqué the lace pieces to a backing and quilt to accent the design.

Cut out the fabric center of a lace-edged doily to make a picture frame, or mount a picture on top of a doily. Lacy frames would be especially appropriate for ancestral pictures or to show off the picture of a new baby.

Many of the pillowcases found in trunks and attics are trimmed with lace; some are also embellished with embroidery. They can be opened out and re-made into other items, or the lace edging can be removed and used again.

Suitable handkerchiefs could be appliquéd to background squares, which are then connected with contrasting strips of fabric to make a quilt top. For another effect, mount the handkerchiefs whole on a soft, colored background, overlapping crazy quilt style, using lace and ribbons to trim.

Make a nostalgic quilt top for a baby's crib or a full-sized bed by cutting handkerchiefs in heart shapes, using the decorated corner as the point of the heart, and appliquéing them to a background that shows off the patterns.

Lacy corners of handkerchiefs were cut into heart shapes and appliquéd on red fabric to make a baby quilt.

Handkerchiefs cut so the decorated corners are in kite-shaped pieces can be pieced together into a "grandmother's fan" quilt pattern.

Individual medallions are often found among attic treasures. These may have been made as samples to try out different patterns before deciding which to use, to add to a collection of patterns for possible future use, or to learn new techniques. They may have been the beginning of an abandoned large project such as a tablecloth in which the small medallions would have been joined with crochet or needlework, or they could even have been left over after a large project was completed.

These little medallions can be used in many ways. Make an

appliqué picture of a vase of flowers on a table, using a handkerchief for the table cloth and small motifs or medallions as the flowers. They can also be used in fabric pictures as wheels on a baby carriage, snowflakes, Victorian windows on a house, ladies' hats, the moon, or just as design elements. Combine them with other pieces of lace or fabric and add details with embroidery.

A medallion can become the focal point of an outfit if used as an insertion on a yoke or bodice.

Small medallions can be stiffened and shaped to make flower heads on wire stems for a lacy bouquet. Stiffened medallions make lovely ornaments to hang on the Christmas tree. Bits and pieces of lace can be sewed together (or pinned in place) to cover styrofoam balls or eggs for Christmas or Easter ornaments. First cover the forms with colorful satin or wrap with silky thread.

If you have lace items that are only fragments—much too worn to consider repair and of no particular historical or sentimental value, use parts and pieces to make other things. Perhaps a wornout tablecloth could be used to repair a similar one which is not so worn. Cut out motifs and appliqué over tears and worn spots. Or make something smaller, such as a table runner, an apron, or a tunic from a tablecloth. Use worn pieces as you would use yardage, fitting the pattern pieces to show off the lace. Be sure to secure all cut edges which could run or ravel.

Attaching Lace to Fabric

A beautiful example of handcrafted lace representing hours of loving care in its making certainly deserves care and craftsmanship when attaching it to another piece of fabric. The suitability of the fabric to the lace is very important. The fabric to which the lace is attached should be compatible in color, fiber, and texture. If the color cannot be matched exactly, it may be better to use a contrasting color. The thread used to attach the lace to the fabric should be as close as possible in both color and weight to the thread used in making the lace. Another important consideration is suitability to the item's planned use. A garment requiring frequent laundering would need different treatment than a piece which is only used for display.

Most lacemakers feel strongly that a handcrafted piece of lace should be attached to the fabric with hand sewing. The choice of machine vs. hand attachment is a personal decision, and more important than the method is the care and skill of execution. Today's sewing machines have a variety of stitch patterns and adjustments for the length, width, and closeness of the stitches. Careful machine operation and good choice of stitches and thread can produce a result superior to poorly executed handwork, just as beautiful hand stitching can be much more attractive than careless machine stitching. Consider your own talents and decide whether to work by hand or machine, or a combination of both, to achieve the desired result.

Identification Key

The principal lacemaking techniques, classified by their basic construction method, are summarized in the following Key. Examples of typical pieces are shown. Study the piece of lace you wish to identify over a contrasting background, in good light and with a magnifying glass, if the lace is made with fine thread. Try to determine how the threads were manipulated to make the lace.

Compare your lace with the pictures of typical pieces of the different kinds of lace shown in the Key. Of course, it is unlikely that your piece will look exactly like any of the pieces pictured, so study how the threads go and look for general similarities. Find a picture that resembles your lace and then refer to the section in the text that gives detailed information about that kind of lace. If the information in the text does not confirm that your piece of lace is that type, check the Key for another possibility. Page through the book, comparing your piece with all the examples until you find its closest relative. Be alert to the possibility that two or more techniques might be combined in a single piece of lace.

Handmade laces are shown in the first part of the Key. A brief summary of types of machine-made lace is at the end of the Key.

Telling handmade and machine-made laces apart:

Unvarying regularity, repeat after repeat, is an indication that a lace is machine-made. If there are irregularities in a machine-made lace, they appear in the same place in each repeat.

Some machine-made reproductions of bobbin lace exactly duplicate handmade, but usually the woven areas have a different appearance, the footings are different, and two weights of thread may have been used in the machine-made piece where only one would have been used in handmade.

Machine-made reproductions of net darning do not have a knotted net, and filling threads zigzag back and forth between adjacent vertical threads rather than crossing the design area, going over and under the threads of the net.

Machine-knit laces have threads looping across to adjacent vertical rows of loops.

In machine embroidery on net the thread does not go over and under the threads of the net. The sewing is like the zigzag stitch of a sewing machine, made with two threads.

Machine-embroidered eyelet and cutwork on woven fabric

Classifying lace by construction method

Looping

Bringing loops of thread through previously formed loops

Includes: Crochet, hairpin lace, broomstick lace, knitting

Knotting

Tying two or more threads together

Includes: Netting, knotted lace (Armenian lace), macrame, waffle work, tatting

Crossing

Passing threads over and under one another by twisting, braiding, and weaving

Includes: Sprang, weaving, interlacing, bobbin lace

Needlework

Making stitches with a threaded needle

Includes: Needlework on net, needlework on woven fabric, needle lace, Tenerife lace, Battenberg lace

have the same number of stitches in any part of each repeat of the design, and the threads cross from one part of the design to another in the same place, which rarely is true in hand embroidery.

Chemical laces (machine-embroidery on a background fabric, which is then removed by chemicals or heat) reproduce the general appearance of needle lace, Irish crochet, tatting, and Battenberg lace, but do not have the characteristic stitches. The threads arc jumbled and the edges of solid areas are fuzzy.

Looping

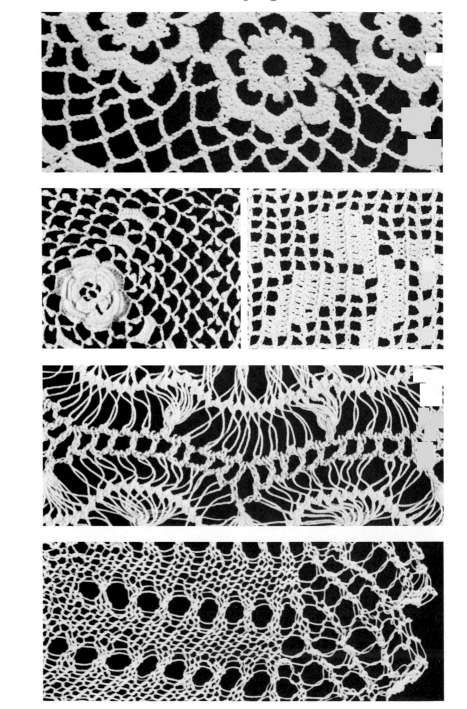

Crochet
page 12

Irish crochet
page 18

Filet crochet
page 21

Hairpin lace
page 25

Knitting
page 32

Knotting

Netting
page 40

Knotted lace
(Armenian lace)
page 44

Macrame
page 46

Waffle work
page 50

Tatting
page 53

Crossing

Sprang
page 62

Weaving
page 66

Interlacing
page 68

Bobbin lace
page 72

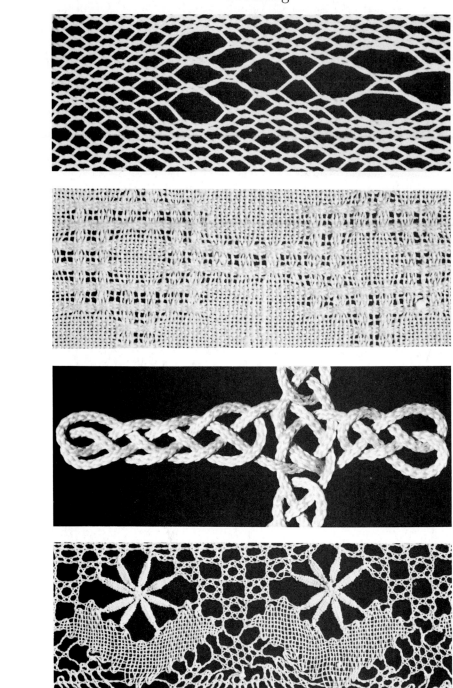

Needlework

Net darning
page 82

Needlework on fine net
(Needle-run)
page 88

Drawnwork
page 95

Hardanger
page 100

Eyelet
page 104

Needlework

Cutwork
page 107

Fagoting
page 111

Needle lace
page 112

Tenerife lace
page 116

Battenberg lace
page 122

Novelty Tapes

Rickrack
page 130

Medallion tape
page 131

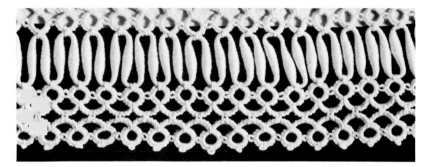

Coronation cord
page 132

Machine-made Lace

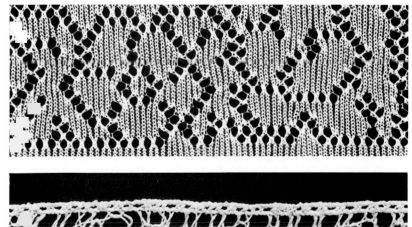

Knitting
page 138

Resembling
bobbin lace
page 139

Machine-made Lace

Resembling
net darning
page 140

Resembling
filet crochet
page 141

Machine embroidery
on fabric
page 144

Machine embroidery
on fabric,
background removed
(chemical lace)
page 145

Machine embroidery
on net
page 146

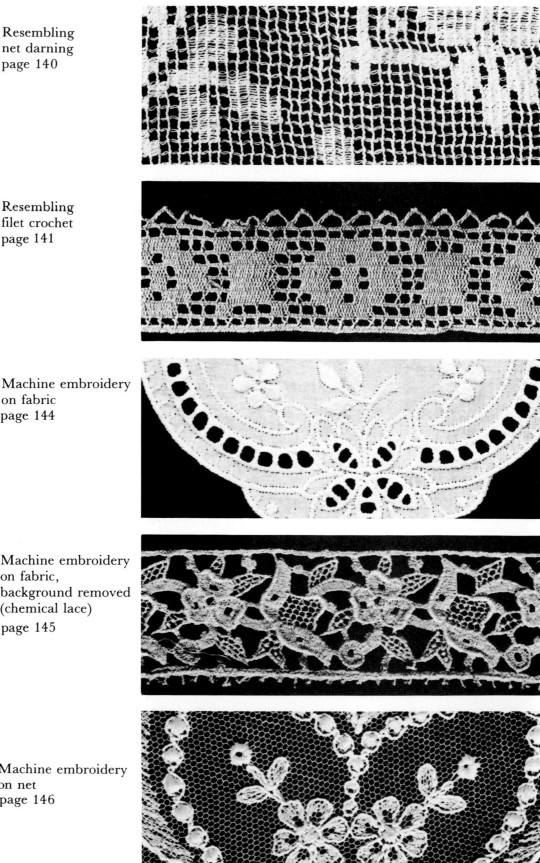

Glossary

Alençon: 1. needle lace made in Alençon, in northwestern France. It has a pronounced cordonet outlining the design areas, which have a clothlike texture, some openwork areas in the pattern, and an hexagonal mesh ground, sometimes dotted. 2. machine-made lace resembling handmade Alençon, frequently used on lingerie

Aloe lace: lace made of fibers of aloe plants (members of the lily family), especially in Italy, Paraguay, the Azores, and the Philippines. The fibers become gummy on contact with water.

Antimacassars: covers, usually decorative, to protect the arms or backs of chairs or sofas (from "anti" + "Macassar," a popular oil hairdressing used in the mid-1800s)

Appliqué: sewing lace motifs or fabric onto net or woven fabric (from the French "to put on" or "apply")

Bars (brides, bridges, legs): threads braided, twisted, overcast, or buttonhole stitched, crossing open spaces between solid parts of lace designs, connecting them and holding them in position

Bertha: a collar, usually lacy, three or four feet long and four to eight inches wide worn around the shoulders leaving the neck and upper chest bare, fashionable from the late 1600s through the 1800s (named for Berthe, eighth-century queen of the Franks, mother of Charlemagne, who was celebrated for her skill in needlework)

Brides: see Bars

Bridges: see Bars

Chantilly lace: 1. bobbin lace, usually black, made at Chantilly in northeastern France, used in large quantities in Spain and Spanish America for shawls and mantillas. Delicate designs of flowers and flowing bands were made in smaller sections and joined invisibly. 2. machine-made reproductions of Chantilly lace

Continuous lace: see Straight lace

Cordonnet (gimp): a heavier thread outlining and defining motifs of a lace pattern

Doily (doyley): originally, a small woven mat, usually fringed, named for a London cloth merchant named D'Oyley in the early 1700s; now a general term for decorative or protective mats, usually round or oval and often lacy.

Edging: lace designed to be attached by one edge only

Elizabethan era: reign of Queen Elizabeth I of England, 1558–1603

Engrêlure: see Footing

Entoilage: see Ground

Entredeux: French term meaning "between two." See Insertion.

Fancywork: general colloquial term covering all forms of decorative needlework and lacemaking

Fascinator: a woman's lightweight, usually lacy, head scarf

Fillings (jours, modes): ornamental and varied stitches that fill enclosed areas in a lace design, such as leaves or flower petals

Flounces: wide (over six inches) edgings, often scalloped, usually pleated or gathered

Footing (engrêlure): straight side of a lace edging that is sewn to other fabric

Free lace: individual motifs are made independently and then joined with bars or mesh ground.

Galloon (also spelled galon): 1. strip of silk and metal lace used to decorate uniforms in the seventeenth century 2. ribbons of wool and silk used for trimming and binding articles of clothing and furniture 3. strip of lace having a scalloped edge at both sides

Gimp: 1. cordonnet 2. an ornamental cord or flat braid used in trimming

Ground (entoilage, reseau): background of bars or mesh joining the motifs of a lace pattern. In French, "entoilage" contains the "toile," or solid portions of the design. Reseau is French for "network."

Guipure: 1. originally, lace with a raised pattern made of narrow strips of thin parchment wound with silk or gold or silver thread. Expensive but not durable. 2. general name for laces with bold designs joined with bars 3. "Machine embroidered guipures" is a general name for chemical laces made with the Schiffli machine 4. "Guipure d'art" was a nineteenth-century name for net darning.

Insertion (entredeux): strip of lace, usually with two straight edges, to be sewed between two pieces of fabric. A medallion sewed into a cutout area is also called an insertion.

Jabot: decorative, lacy frill worn at the neck of a blouse or dress. In the l8th century, a jabot was a fall of lace or cloth attached to the front of a neckband, worn by men.

Jours: see Fillings

Legs: see Bars

Limerick lace: embroidered net made at Limerick in southwestern Ireland, using both tambour and needle-run techniques. The lace is noted for its wide variety of delicate fillings.

Medallion: a design unit, usually round, oval, square, or hexagonal, which may be used by itself or combined with similar units to make a border or allover design (from the French word meaning "large medal")

Mesh: network, either a single space surrounded by threads or the entire ground. The gauge used in netting was also called a mesh.

Motif: an individual design element or a portion, often recurring, of a larger pattern, such as a flower or a spray of leaves

Net: open fabric in which threads outline square, diamond, hexagonal, or octagonal spaces

Normandy lace: see Patchwork lace

Nottingham lace: machine-made lace produced in Nottingham, England. The stocking frame and warp frame, and the bobbinet, Pusher, Levers, and lace curtain machines were all developed in the Nottingham area.

Overcasting: straight stitches worked over the edge of a piece of cloth or wrapped around a group of threads

Patchwork lace (Normandy lace): different types and patterns of lace, both hand- and machine-made, sewed together in an organized design or a "crazy quilt" effect. Articles such as collars and jabots were made by joining several insertions and an edging. Medallions and areas of plain or tucked net were often included.

Pina cloth: crisp, lightweight, translucent pale yellow cloth made of fibers from the pineapple plant, used in the Philippines for very fine drawnwork

Pita lace: lace made of fibers from the agave, or century plant

Point: from the French word for "stitch," originally referred to lace made with a needle, then to any fine quality lace

Re-embroidered lace: lace in which the design is outlined, emphasized, or embellished with needlework

Reseau: see Ground

Sacque: an infant's short jacket, fastening at the neck

Scallop: an ornamental edging of semicircles (from the shape of the scallop shell)

Sham: a decorative cover for bed pillows, used during the day before it became fashionable to have bedspreads long enough to cover the pillows

Splasher: a piece of fabric, usually decorative, fastened to the wall behind a washstand

St. Gall lace: lace made on Schiffli machines at Saint Gall (Gallen) in northeastern Switzerland

Stiletto: a pointed instrument for piercing holes for eyelet embroidery, usually made of ivory, metal, or wood

Straight laces (continuous laces): laces in which the ground and design elements are worked in one piece (compare with free lace)

Tidies: pieces of fancywork used to protect the backs and arms of chairs and sofas from wear or soil

Toilé: solid areas of a lace design (from the French word for cloth or linen)

Tulle: a very fine, sheer net made of silk, cotton, or synthetic fibers

Valenciennes ("Val") lace: 1. a straight bobbin lace that originated in the town of Valenciennes on the border of France and Flanders (Belgium). It was an expensive lace, made with extremely fine linen thread, using a large number of bobbins. Distinguishing characteristics are a diamond or round braided mesh ground and a line of tiny holes around the design motifs. 2. a general name for narrow machine-made lace edgings and insertions made with fine thread.

Vandyke: deeply indented V-shape decorative edges. Wide collars with V-edges were beautifully painted by the Flemish artist Sir Anthony Van Dyke in portraits of Charles I of England (ruled 1625–1649) and his court. Trim pointed beards appeared in many of these portraits; they also are named for this painter.

Venetian lace: 1. needle lace made in Venice, Italy. In seventeenth-century *point de Venise,* the design elements are so heavily padded they look like carved ivory. Other types of Venetian needle laces are *rose point* (not so heavy as gros point), *point de neige* (with small layered flowers and elaborate picot-like snowflakes), *coraline* (resembling branched coral), and *point plat* (flat, no padding).
2. chemical lace made on the Schiffli machine, reproducing the designs and general appearance but not the stitches of handmade Venetian lace

Victorian era: reign of Queen Victoria of Great Britain, 1837–1901

Warp: lengthwise threads on a loom and in woven fabric

Weft: see Woof

Woof (weft): threads that cross the warp in a woven fabric

Yak lace: a woolen bobbin lace made in the English Midlands in the latter part of the nineteenth century, usually in torchon and Cluny patterns. Despite its name, the wool came from Yorkshire sheep.

Bibliography

This bibliography lists selected publications helpful for lace identification, lacemaking techniques, history of lace, and the care, preservation, and use of lace.

Look for older books in libraries and secondhand bookstores. Needlework magazines from the early 1900s are invaluable references describing lacemaking techniques and showing articles made with these techniques. Look in needlecraft shops for current booklets with directions and designs for specific lacemaking techniques, and check the book lists from lace supply firms for other publications.

GENERAL

Anchor Manual of Needlework. 4th ed. J. and P. Coats Ltd. Newton, MA: Charles T. Branford Company, 1970.
  Directions and patterns for many types of needlework, including attaching lace, eyelet, cutwork, drawnwork, Hardanger, blackwork, shadow work, embroidery on net, tatting, macrame, Tenerife lace, knotted lace, netting, needle lace, Battenberg lace, bobbin lace, crocheting, and knitting.

Bath, Virginia Churchill. *Lace*. Chicago: Henry Regnery Company, 1974.
  History of the principal types of lace, with emphasis on needle lace and bobbin lace. Clear directions with modern applications are given for these and also for netting, darned net, macrame, drawnwork, Tenerife lace, knotted lace, and mixed laces (needlework on net and Battenberg lace).

Bullock, Alice-May. *Lace and Lace Making*. New York: Larousse & Co., Inc., 1981.
  History and identification of lace, with emphasis on bobbin lace, and some information about needle lace, tatting, macrame, tambour and net laces, net darning, knitted lace, crochet, Ayrshire work, Tenerife lace, drawnwork, and machine-made lace.

Caulfeild, S.F.A., and Saward, Blanche C. *Encyclopedia of Victorian Needlework*. Republication (6 vols. in 2) of *The Dictionary of Needlework*, 2nd ed. London, 1887. New York: Dover Publications, Inc., 1972.
  Definitions, history, and instructions for all types of needlework popular in the late 1800s, including 158 pages of 1880s needlework designs.

de Dillmont, Thérèse. *Encyclopedia of Needlework*. D.M.C. Library. Mullhouse, France, n.d. Republication, Philadelphia: Running Press, 1978.
  First written in the 1880s, reprinted many times in many languages, this is the classic how-to book for Victorian needlework. Includes knitting, crochet, hairpin lace, tatting, macrame, netting, net darning, openwork embroidery, embroidery and appliqué on net, needle lace, Tenerife lace, knotted lace, and bobbin lace.

Guild, Vera P. *Good Housekeeping New Complete Book of Needlecraft*. New York: Good Housekeeping Books, 1971.
  Includes directions for knotted lace, Hardanger, cutwork, drawnwork, cross-stitch on gingham, Tenerife embroidery, eyelet, needle weaving, fagoting, knitting, crochet, hairpin lace, tatting, netting, macrame, and hand weaving.

Gastelow, Mary, ed. *The Complete Guide to Needlework*. Secaucus, NJ: Chartwell Books, Inc., 1982.
  History and techniques of needlework, including drawnwork, eyelet, cutwork, Handanger, and Hedebo, with a section on collecting, displaying, and conservation of fabrics.

Hilton, Beverly, ed. *Golden Hands*. 6 vols. New York: Greystone Press, 1973.
  Material first published in the handcraft periodical Golden Hands. Includes instructions and patterns for knitting, crochet, hairpin lace, blackwork, cutwork, drawnwork, insertions, shadow work, tatting, bobbin lace, needle lace, embroidery on square and fine net, netting, macrame, and Tenerife lace.

Howard, Constance, ed. *Textile Crafts*. New York: Charles Scribner's Sons, 1978.
  Chapters written by experts in their fields, including blackwork, drawnwork, sprang, weaving, crochet, knitting, bobbin lace, and macrame.

Lace Guild (England). Hall, Dorothea, ed. *The Gentle Arts*. New York: Exeter Books, 1986.
  Instructions and projects in needle lace, bobbin lace, tatting, knitted lace, crocheted lace, and filet crochet.

Lane, Rose Wilder. *Woman's Day Book of American Needlework*. New York: Simon and Schuster, 1963.
  A collection of articles originally published in *Woman's Day* magazine; includes history, examples, and directions for embroidery, crochet, and knitting.

Longhurst, Denise. *Vanishing American Needle Arts*. New York: G. P. Putnam's Sons, 1984.
  Includes directions for needle lace, cutwork, Hardanger, Hedebo, netting, tatting, and Tenerife lace.

McCall's Big Book of Needlecrafts by the editors of *McCall's Needlework & Crafts Magazines*. Radnor, PA: Chilton Book Company, 1982.
  Includes directions for cutwork, drawnwork, fagoting, Hardanger, embroidery on net, punch stitch, and Tenerife embroidery.

McCall's Needlework Treasury: A Learn and Make Book by the editors of *McCall's Needlework and Crafts Magazine*. New York: Random House-McCall's, 1963.
  Directions for popular and traditional needlecrafts, including punch stitch, cutwork, drawnwork, Tenerife embroidery,

Hardanger, fagoting, embroidery on net, cross-stitch on gingham, hairpin lace, knitting, crochet, tatting, netting, net darning, bobbin lace, and braiding.

Olde Time Needlework (magazine). Seabrook, NH: The House of White Birches/Tower Press. Published several times a year 1972–82, as a yearly special 1982-86.
   Magazine containing reprints of directions and patterns for many types of needlework from the Victorian era to the present time.

Pfannschmidt, Ernst Erik. *Twentieth Century Lace.* New York: Charles Scribners' Sons, 1975.
   History, structure, and contempory designs in lace.

Reader's Digest Complete Guide to Needlework. Pleasantville, NY: The Reader's Digest Association, Inc., 1979.
   Directions for popular needlecrafts, including blackwork, drawnwork, Hardanger, cutwork, knitting, crochet, needle lace, tatting, net darning, bobbin lace, hand weaving, hairpin lace, and macrame.

Ryan, Mildred Graves. *The Complete Encyclopedia of Stitchery.* New York: New American Library, 1979.
   Instructions for crochet, filet crochet, Irish crochet, hairpin lace, blackwork, eyelet, cutwork, drawnwork, Hardanger, Hedebo, machine embroidery, needle weaving, net embroidery, shadow work, tambour, Tenerife embroidery, knitting, macrame, and tatting.

Waller, Irene. *Designing with Thread: From Fiber to Fabric.* New York: The Viking Press, 1973.
   Exploration of techniques used in various methods of fabric construction, including netting, macrame, tatting, hand and machine knitting, crochet, weaving, sprang, bobbin lace, and machine-made laces.

Warren, Mrs., and Pullman (Pullan), Mrs. *Treasures in Needlework.* London, 1870. Reprint. New York: Berkley Publishing Corporation, 1976.
   Instructions that had been published in the Needlework Department of the British magazine *Family Friend*, including knitting, netting, net darning, crochet, tape lace, tatting, and embroidery.

BOBBIN LACE

Collier, Ann. *Creative Design in Bobbin Lace.* Newton, MA: Charles T. Branford Company, 1982.
   Instructions for making bobbin lace and adapting basic techniques in imaginative designs.

Cook, Bridget M. *Practical Skills in Bobbin Lace.* New York: Dover Publications, Inc., 1987.
   Detailed instructions with over 700 diagrams explaining specific bobbin lace techniques.

Dye, Gilian. *Beginning Bobbin Lace.* London: Dryad Press Ltd., 1986. Reprint. New York, Dover Publications, Inc., 1987.
   Instructions in basic bobbin lace for beginning lacemakers.

Dye, Gilian. *Bobbin Lace Braid.* Newton Center, MA: Charles T. Branford Co., 1979.
   Instructions for making bobbin lace, starting with simple braids.

Fuhrmann, Brigita. *Bobbin Lace: An Illustrated Guide to Traditional and Contemporary Techniques.* Republication of *Bobbin Lace: A Contemporary Approach.* 1976. New York: Dover Publications, Inc., 1985.
   History, instructions for making bobbin lace, and adapting basic techniques to innovative designs.

Hopewell, Jeffery. *Pillow Lace and Bobbins.* Shire Album No. 9. 2nd ed. Aylesbury, Bucks, England: Shire Publications Ltd., 1984.
   Booklet illustrating types of English bobbin lace and lace-making equipment, with pictures of more than 90 different lace bobbins.

Kliot, Kaethe and Jules. *Bobbin Lace: Form by the Twisting of Cords.* New York: Crown Publishers, Inc., 1973.
   History, techniques, and modern applications of bobbin lace.

Luxton, Elsie. *The Technique of Honiton Lace.* Newton, MA: Charles T. Branford Company, 1979.
   Instructions for Honiton bobbin lace, from beginner's level to expert.

Maidment, Margaret. *A Manual of Hand-Made Bobbin Lace Work.* England, 1931. Republication. McMinville, OR: Robin and Russ Handweavers, 1983.
   History and descriptions of the distinctive laces of the various English lacemaking areas, emphasizing the technical details of the stitches and methods used.

Mincoff, Elizabeth, and Marriage, Margaret S. *Pillow or Bobbin Lace: Techniques, Patterns, History.* Republication of *Pillow Lace: A Practical Hand-Book*, 1907. New York: Dover Publications, Inc., 1987.
   History of bobbin lace, with patterns and instructions for fifty lace designs.

Nottingham, Pamela. *Bobbin Lace Making.* London: B. T. Batsford, 1983.
   Bucks Point Lace-making. London: B. T. Batsford, 1986.
   The Technique of Bobbin Lace. London: B. T. Batsford, 1976.
   The Technique of Bucks Point Lace. London: B. T. Batsford, 1981.
   The Technique of Torchon Lace. Corvallis, OR: Robin and Russ Handweavers, 1980.
   Instructions for making different types of English bobbin lace.

Southard, Doris. *Bobbin Lacemaking.* New York: Charles Scribner's Sons, 1977.
   History, equipment, and instructions for basic bobbin lace techniques.

CONSERVATION

Collins, Maureen. *How To Wet-Clean Undyed Cotton and Linen.* Smithsonian Institution, Museum of History and Technology, Textile Laboratory, Information Leaflet 478. Washington, D.C.: Smithsonian Institution, 1967.
   Leaflet describing recommended cleaning methods that are suitable for most laces.

Diez, Ruth, Betty Feather, Sherri Johnson, and Marjorie Sohn. *Stain Removal for Washable Fabrics.* North Central Region Extension Publication 64. 1979.

Hamilton, Audie. Nong, Melisa Hamilton, ed. *Textiles, Home Care and Conservation.* Corpus Christi, TX: by the author, P.O. Box 260155, 78426-0155, 1984.
   Booklet with basic information for the nonspecialist on cleaning, storing, displaying, and conserving textiles.

Laundering Factsheet Notebook. Soap and Detergent Association Consumer Affairs Committee, 475 Park Ave. South, New York, NY 10016.

Leene, Jenita E., ed. *Textile Conservation*. Washington, D.C.: Smithsonian Institution, 1972.
Recommendations for cleaning, restoring, and preserving all types of textiles.

Mailand, Harold F. *Considerations for the Care of Textiles and Costumes, a Handbook for the Non-Specialist*. Indianapolis, IN: Indianapolis Museum of Arts, 1980.
Booklet of instructions for cleaning, storing, and displaying fabrics.

HISTORY

May, Florence Lewis. *Hispanic Lace and Lace Making*. 1939. Reprint. New York: The Hispanic Society of America, 1980.
History of the types of lace made in various parts of Spain and Portugal and in the Azores, Philippine Islands, Mexico, South and Central America. Illustrations of laces and costumes.

Mushena, Elizabeth J. *Book of Colonial Needlework*. New York: Van Nostrand Reinhold Company, 1975.
History of colonial needlework with directions for modern applications, including openwork and whitework embroidery.

Pallister, Mrs. Bury. *History of Lace*. Republication of the 4th ed., 1911. New York: Dover Publications, Inc., 1984.
Written in the 1870s, revised and expanded in 1901. Has been called the definitive history of lacemaking. Describes and illustrates the types of lace made in each European country.

Swan, Susan Burrows. *Plain & Fancy: American Women and Their Needlework*. New York: Holt, Rinehart and Winston, 1977.
History of "plain sewing" and "fancy needlework" done by American women from 1700 to 1850.

Vinciolo, Federico. *Renaissance Patterns for Lace, Embroidery and Needlepoint*. Republication of 1909 edition of *Singuliers et nouveaux pourtraicts*, first published in 1587. New York: Dover Publications, Inc., 1971.
Designs for needle lace and net darning that set the styles during the sixteenth century.

IDENTIFICATION and DEFINITIONS

Earnshaw, Pat. *Bobbin & Needle Laces, Identification and Care*. McMinnville, OR: Robin and Russ Handweavers, 1983.
Identification of bobbin and needle laces, and how to distinguish them from embroidered and machine-made laces, with chapters on cleaning, storing, and displaying lace.

A Dictionary of Lace. Aylesbury, Bucks, England: Shire Publications Ltd., 1982.
Definitions of over 400 terms relating to lace, history, and photographs of laces, costumes, and lacemaking machines.

_____. *The Identification of Lace*. Aylesbury, Bucks, England: Shire Publications Ltd., 1980.
History and identification of embroidered, needle, and bobbin laces, with a section on "machine laces and other 'imitation' laces."

Eveleth, E. Lolita. *Chart for Lace Identification and the Meshes of Handmade Lace*. An International Old Lacers Inc. publication. Westfield, MA: The Sterling Press, Inc., 1974.
Booklet with information about and pictures of bobbin laces, needle laces, and miscellaneous laces, and enlarged pictures of bobbin and needle lace meshes.

Jackson, Emily (Mrs. F. Nevill). *Old Handmade Lace, With a Dictionary of Lace*. London, 1900. Republication. New York: Dover Publications, Inc., 1987.
History and identification of handmade laces, with a dictionary and glossary of lace terms.

Kliot, Jules and Kaethe. "Looking at Lace." *Fiber Arts*, May/June 1982, pp. 43–49.
Identifying laces, classified as true laces (needle and bobbin lace), popular handmade laces (single thread and multiple thread), and machine-made laces.

Mills, Betty J. *The Language of Lace*. Lubbock, TX: Texas Tech University (Vintage Press, Inc.), 1984.
Booklet summarizing lace history and types of lace, with examples of needle laces, bobbin laces, decorated net laces, tape lace, machine laces, and craft and imitation laces.

KNOTTING and INTERLACEMENTS

Bain, George. *Celtic Art: the Methods of Construction*. Glasgow, Scotland, 1951. Republication. New York: Dover Publications, Inc., 1973.
A source book of Celtic knotwork and interlacement designs.

Cheng, Lydia, and the editors of Echo Books. *Chinese Knotting*. 2nd English ed. Taipei, Taiwan: Echo Publishing Company Ltd., 1986. Distributed by Charles E. Tuttle.
History, symbolic connotations, and construction of traditional Chinese knots, with examples of contemporary applications.

Groumount, Raoul, and Wenstrom, Elmer. *Square Knotting or Macrame: Square Knot Handicraft Guide*. New York: Cornell Maritime Press, Inc., 1949. Distributed by Random House.
Photographs and diagrams of useful and ornamental knots and braids, including cross clove hitch work (waffle work) and netting.

Harvey, Virginia I. *Macrame: the Art of Creative Knotting*. Rev. ed. New York: Van Nostrand Reinhold Book Corporation, 1986.
Instructions for the basic knots used in macrame, with photographs and diagrams of how they can be used in a wide variety of patterns.

Kasparian, Alice Odian. *Armenian Needlelace and Armenian Embroidery*. McLean, VA: EMP Publications, 1983.
History, examples, and directions for Armenian lace.

The Macrame Book. Seabrook, NH: The House of White Birches, 1981.
Booklet, republication of instructions and designs for macrame projects, from the early 1900s.

Meilach, Dona Z. *Macrame, Creative Design in Knotting*. New York: Crown Publishers, Inc., 1971.
Instructions for basic and advanced macrame, showing a wide range of contemporary applications.

The Netting Book. Seabrook, NH: Tower Press, 1981.
Booklet, republication of directions for netting and net darning, from the early 1900s.

Shaw, George Russell. *Knots, Useful and Ornamental*. 3rd ed. New York: Macmillan, 1972.
Diagrams of knot used in macrame, netting, and tatting, Chinese and Celtic knots and interlacements, Japanese knots, and braiding.

Tashjian, Nouvart. Kliot, Jules and Kaethe, eds. *Armenian Lace*. Republication of *The Priscilla Armenian Needlepoint Lace Book*, 1923. Berkeley, CA: Lacis Publications, 1982.
Booklet of instructions for making Armenian knotted lace, showing many examples.

Walker, Louisa. *Graded Lessons in Macrame, Knotting and Netting.* Republication of *Varied Occupations in String Work.* London, 1896. New York: Dover Publications, Inc., 1971.

Instructions for various knotwork projects, including braids, netting, hairpin lace, and macrame.

LOOPING—CROCHET and KNITTING

Blackwell, Liz. *A Treasury of Crochet Patterns.* New York: Charles Scribner's Sons, 1971.

Directions for nearly 400 crochet stitches and patterns.

de Dillmont, Thérèse, Ed. *Masterpieces of Irish Crochet Lace.* Abridged republication of *Irish Crochet Lace.* France, early 1900s. New York: Dover Publications, Inc., 1986.

Instructions for motifs and grounds used by skilled makers of Irish crochet lace in the late 19th century.

Horne, Patience, and Bowden, Stephen. *Paton's Book of Knitting and Crochet.* Boston: Little, Brown and Company, 1973.

History, materials, techniques, and instructions for knitting and crochet.

Goldberg, Rhoda Ochser. *The New Crochet Dictionary.* New York: Crown Publishers, Inc., 1986.

Basic how to, definitions, and directions for dozens of crochet stitches, medallions, and edgings; includes filet crochet, hairpin lace, broomstick lace, and loop stitches.

Kinzel, Marianne. *First Book of Modern Lace Knitting.* England, 1954. Republication. New York: Dover Publications, Inc., 1972.

Instructions for round and square lace knitting, in words and charts.

———. *Second Book of Modern Lace Knitting.* England, 1961. Republication. New York: Dover Publications, Inc., 1972.

Additional round and square lace knitting patterns in words and charts.

Orr, Anne. *Crochet Designs of Anne Orr.* New York: Dover Publications, Inc., 1978.

Booklet of collected designs by Anne Orr first published in the early 1900s.

Priscilla Publishing Co. *Irish Crochet: Techniques and Projects.* Republication of *Priscilla Irish Crochet Book,* 1909. New York: Dover Publications, Inc., 1984.

Instructions for simple and complex projects in Irish crochet.

Waldrep, Mary Carolyn. *Crocheting Collars, Cuffs and Yokes.* New York: Dover Publications, Inc., 1987.

Booklet of patterns from instruction leaflets published by thread companies in the 1910s to 1950s.

———. *Floral Crochet.* New York: Dover Publications, Inc., 1987.

Booklet of patterns for doilies, edgings, tablecloths, and bedspreads from instruction leaflets published by thread companies in the 1940s and 1950s.

Weinstein, Florence, ed. *Crocheting Tablecloths and Placemats.* New York: Dover Publications, Inc., 1975.

Collection of crochet patterns originally published between 1937 and 1944.

Weis, Rita, ed. *Crocheting Doilies.* 1976.
Crocheting Edgings. 1980.
Crocheting Placemats. 1978.
Favorite Crocheted Placemat Designs. 1985.
Favorite Filet Crochet Designs. 1985.
Favorite Irish Crochet Designs. 1985.
Heirloom Crochet Designs. 1987.
Pineapple Crochet Designs. 1985.
Traditional Edgings to Crochet. 1987.

New York: Dover Publications, Inc.

Booklets of collected designs first published in the early 1900s.

Weldon and Company. *Victorian Crochet.* Republication of *Weldon's Practical Crochet.* London, 1895. New York: Dover Publications, Inc., 1974.

Patterns for all types of crochet and hairpin lace projects from the Victorian era, originally published as a series of newsletters.

MACHINE LACE

Earnshaw, Pat. *Lace Machines and Machine Lace.* London: B. T. Batsford Ltd., 1986.

Comprehensive history of the development of lace machines, with detailed descriptions of how they operate and pictures of the laces made on them.

Halls, Zillah. *Machine-made Lace in Nottingham,* 2nd ed. Nottingham England: Nottingham Printers Limited, 1981.

Booklet outlining the development of lacemaking machines in the Nottingham area.

Singer Sewing Machine Company. Kliot, Jules and Kaethe, eds. *Singer Instructions for Art Embroidery and Lace Work.* 7th ed. 1941. Republication. Berkeley, CA: Lacis Publications, 1987.

Instructions for interpreting a wide variety of lacemaking techniques using the straight-stitch, treadle sewing machine, without attachments.

NEEDLEWORK—GENERAL

Ambuter, Carolyn. *The Open Canvas: An Instructional Encyclopedia of Openwork Techniques.* New York: Workman Publishing, 1982.

Includes directions for drawnwork, needle weaving, hem-stitching, net darning, Hardanger, Hedebo, and needle lace.

Cadovius, Jacqueline. *Net Darning Lace.* Closter, NJ: JES Handicrafts, 1982.

Booklet of instructions and patterns for net darning projects using woven net.

Cave, Oenome. *Cut-Work Embroidery and How to Do It.* Revised republication of *Linen Cut-Work.* London, 1963. New York: Dover Publications, Inc., 1982.

History and directions for cutwork, drawnwork, and needle lace.

Lovesey, Nenia. *Introduction to Needlepoint Lace.* New York: Larousse & Co., Inc., 1985.

History, identification, and instructions for needle lace.

———. *The Technique of Needlepoint Lace.* New York: Larousse & Co., Inc., 1980.

History, descriptions, and instructions for needle lace, Tenerife lace, netting, Carrickmacross, tambour, and needle-run lace.

Nielsen, Edith. *Scandinavian Embroidery: Past and Present.* New York: Charles Scribner's Sons, 1978.

History, examples, and directions for Scandinavian embroidery, including Hardanger, Hedebo, blackwork, drawnwork, cutwork, and eyelet.

Nordfors, Jill. *Needle Lace and Needleweaving.* Livermore, CA: Aardvark Adventures, 1985.

Directions for the stitches used in needle lace and needle weaving, with illustrations of traditional and contempory applications.

Preston, Doris Campbell. *Needle-made Laces and Net Embroideries.* London, 1938. Reprint. New York: Dover Publications, Inc., 1984.

History and directions for needlework on net (needlerun, tambour, and Carrickmacross), Irish crochet, needle lace, Battenberg, net darning, and tatting.

Prickett, Elizabeth. *Ruskin Lace & Linen Work*. London: B. T. Batsford, 1985. Reprint. New York: Dover Publications, Inc., 1986.
 Instructions and patterns for a type of openwork embroidery incorporating drawnwork, cutwork, and needle lace, developed in the English lake district in the late 1800s.

Thomas, Mary. *Mary Thomas's Embroidery Book*, 1936. Republication. New York: Dover Publications, Inc., 1983.
 Shows the stitches used in different types of needlework, including blackwork, drawnwork, eyelet, cutwork, net darning, Hardanger, Hedebo, needle weaving, net embroidery, and shadow work.

Weis, Rita. *Treasury of Designs for Lace Net Embroidery*. New York: Dover Publications, Inc., 1985.
 Booklet of collected designs first published in the early 1900s.

Wilson, Erica. *The Craft of Black Work and White Work*. New York: Charles Scribner's Sons, 1973.
 History, instructions, and designs for blackwork and for Hardanger, drawnwork, needle weaving, eyelet, shadow work, embroidery on net, and Battenberg lace.

NEEDLEWORK — BATTENBERG

Brown, Nellie Clark. Kliot, Jules and Kaethe, eds. *Battenberg and Point Lace Book*, 2nd ed. Republication of *The Priscilla Battenberg and Point Lace Book*, 1912. Berkeley, CA: Lacis Publications, 1987.
 First printed near the end of the period when Battenberg lace was most popular, the book was a compilation of earlier publications. This edition also illustrates over 100 Battenberg patterns currently available for articles such as doilies, collars, yokes, and handkerchiefs, and contains updated information on construction and care.

Eaton, Ethel A., and Denton, Edna L. *The Story of Battenberg Lace*. Portland, OR: by the authors, 5412 N.E. 24th Ave, 97211, 1970.
 Booklet of history, directions, and patterns for Battenberg lace.

How to Make Battenberg and Point Lace. Seabrook, NH: The House of White Birches, 1981.
 Republication of a booklet of instructions and stitches for Battenberg lace, from the early 1900s.

Kliot, Jules and Kaethe, eds. *Needle Laces: Battenberg, Point & Reticella*. Berkley, CA: Lacis Publications, 1981.
 Booklet of collected instructions, stitches, and patterns published between 1878 and 1938.

NEEDLEWORK — DRAWNWORK

The Art of Drawn Work. Seabrook, NH: Tower Press, Inc., 1981.
 Booklet of detailed instructions for drawnwork, reprinted from the early 1900s; includes several macrame fringes.

Drysdale, Rosemary. *Pulled Work on Canvas and Linen*. New York: Charles Scribner's Sons, 1978.
 Over 100 openwork patterns made by pulling fabric threads together with stitches.

Fangel, Ester; Winkler, Ida; and Madsen, Agnette Wuldem. *Danish Pulled Thread Embroidery*. Republication of parts 3 and 4 of *Danish Embroidery*, 1959. New York: Dover Publications, Inc., 1977.
 Traditional designs for Danish pulled thread work (drawnwork), with English and Danish text.

John, Edith. *Needleweaving*. Newton, MA: Charles T. Branford Company, 1970.
 Instructions for and modern applications of needle weaving.

McNeill, Moyra. *Drawn Fabric*. Needlecraft Series #8. Tumbridge Wells, Kent, England: Search Press Limited, 1984.
 Booklet of directions for making openwork patterns by tightly pulling certain stitches.

NEEDLEWORK — HARDANGER

Bright, Sigrid. *Hardanger Embroidery*. Republication of *Hardanger Book*, early 1900s. New York: Dover Publications, Inc., 1978.
 Booklet of instructions and patterns for Hardanger embroidery.

Priscilla Publishing Company. *Traditional Hardanger Embroidery*. Republication of *Priscilla Hardanger Book No. 2: A Collection of Typical Norwegian Designs*, 1924. New York: Dover Publications, Inc., 1984.
 Booklet with directions for 50 traditional Hardanger designs.

NEEDLEWORK — TENERIFE LACE

Kaiser, Eunice Gifford. *Enjoy Making Tenerife and Other Lace*. Odessa, TX: Kaiser Crafts, 1981.
 Instructions for Tenerife lace, needle lace, and Battenberg lace, with directions for making tapes of bobbin lace, tatting, hairpin lace, crochet, and macrame for Battenberg lace.

Kliot, Jules and Kaethe, eds. *Tenerife Lace*. Berkeley, CA: Lacis Publications, 1986.
 Republication of four manuals with instructions and patterns printed in the early 1900s, plus suggestions for adapting contemporary materials.

Stillwell, Alexandra. *The Technique of Tenerife Lace*. Watertown, MA: Charles T. Branford Co., 1980.
 Instructions for making traditional Tenerife lace motifs, braids, and shaped articles, with contemporary applications.

SPRANG/WEAVING

Andrews, Denison. *How to Make Your Own Hammock and Lie in It*. 2nd ed. New York: Workman Publishing Company, 1978.
 Booklet that includes directions for making hammocks by looped netting and sprang.

Collingwood, Peter. *The Techniques of Sprang*. New York: Watson Guptill Publications, 1974.
 History and directions for basic sprang and many variations.

Held, Shirley E. *Weaving: a Handbook for Fiber Craftsmen*. 2nd ed. New York: Holt, Rinehart and Winston, Inc., 1973.
 History of fiber crafts, descriptions of materials, equipment, and techniques of weaving, including sections on macrame, sprang, netting, and lace weaves.

Kliot, Jules. *Sprang: Language and Techniques*. 2nd ed. Berkeley, CA: Some Place Publications, 1979.
 Booklet of instructions for basic sprang and variations.

Skowronski, Hella, and Reddy, Mary. *Sprang: Thread Twisting, A Creative Technique*. New York: Van Nostrand Reinhold Company, 1974.
 Instructions for a wide variety of sprang twists, and suggestions for using sprang textiles in clothing and decoration.

TATTING

Auld, Rhoda L. *Tatting: The Contemporary Art of Knotting with a Shuttle*. New York: Van Nostrand Reinhold Company, 1974.
    History, instructions, tools, and materials for contemporary work, design, and color in tatting.

Hahn, Monica. *A Christmas Angel — Volume II — and Other Tatting Patterns*. Seattle, WA: By the author, 822 N.E. 91st, 98115, 1985.
    Booklet of tatting patterns; including directions for twisted stitch, Cluny tatting, and heart-rings.

Jones, Rebecca. *The Complete Book of Tatting*. London: Dryad Press Limited, 1985.
    History, materials, instructions (for six methods of tatting), and patterns, traditional and contemporary.

Kuhn, Mary Sue. *The Joy of Tatting*. Des Moines, Iowa: Published by the author, P.O. Box 65072, 50265, 1979.
    History, how to tat, using small motifs, making dimensional flowers, using old pieces, and working with new fibers.

Morgan, Lael. *Tatting: A New Look at the Old Art of Making Lace*. Garden City, NY: Doubleday & Company, Inc., 1977.
    History and directions for tatting traditional patterns and for using heavier threads in modern applications.

Nicholls, Elgiva. *Tatting: Technique & History*. London, 1962. Republication. New York: Dover Publications, Inc., 1984.
    Historical development of tatting, with instructions for using the basic elements in making unusual designs.

Orr, Anne. *Anne Orr's Classic Tatting Patterns*. Republication. *Tatting, Book #5* (Revised), 1940. New York: Dover Publications, Inc., 1985.
    Booklet of collected designs by Anne Orr first published in the early 1900s.

Rodgers, Kemis C., ed. *Olde Time Tatting*. Seabrook, NH: The House of White Birches, 1982.
    Booklet of instructions, history, and patterns for tatting. Includes instructions for twisted stitch, beaded tatting, tatted netting, and tatting combined with coronation cord.

Sanders, Julia E. *Tatting Patterns*. Republication of *The Priscilla Tatting Book No. 2. A Collection of Beautiful and Useful Patterns with Directions for Working*, 1915. New York: Dover Publications, Inc., 1977.
    Instructions for making a wide variety of projects, including patterns with beads and coronation cord.

Weis, Rita, ed. *Tatted Doilies and Edgings*. 1980. *Traditional Tatting Patterns*. 1986. New York: Dover Publications, Inc.
    Booklets of collected designs first published in the early 1900s.

USING LACE

Laury, Jean Ray. *New Uses for Old Laces*. Garden City, NJ: Doubleday & Company, Inc., 1974.
    Suggestions for mounting lace pieces for display and for using old laces for collages, clothing, quilts, etc.

Wilson, Erica. *Needlework to Wear*. Birmingham, AL: Oxmoor House, Inc., 1982.
    Instructions for making items of clothing and accessories using a wide variety of techniques, including macrame, crochet, cutwork, needle lace, and reembroidered lace.

Withers, Jean. *Mounting & Using Lace*. London: Dryad Press, Ltd. 1986.
    Detailed directions for various ways to attach lace to woven fabric or net, with suggestions for ways to use and display lace edgings, insertions, and motifs.

CURRENT PERIODICALS DEVOTED TO LACE:

International Old Lacers, Inc. Bulletin (bimonthly)
    (Membership in IOLI includes Bulletin subscription)
    6903 Windy Ridge Drive, Dallas, TX 75248
    Attn: Skip Diamond, Librarian

Lace Crafts Quarterly
    3201 E. Lakeshore Drive, Tallahassee, FL 32312

Lace Magazine (quarterly)
    Belgium Lace School
    1840 South Gaffey St., San Pedro, CA 90731

Lacemaking Today
    Bizarre Butterfly Publishing
    1347 E. San Miguel, Phoeniz, AZ 85014

Index

Types of lace shown in the room scenes:

Page 10

Sheet, pillowcases, and nightgown case: knitted lace

Tablecloth: ladder cutwork, cutwork with needle lace insets, net darning edging

Child's dress: tatting

Page 38

Tablecloth: drawnwork borders, netted edging

Napkins: ladder cutwork, cutwork with needle lace insets, net darning edging

Page 60

Tablecloth: net darning, cutwork, five patterns of bobbin lace

Bookmark: bobbin lace

Shawl: hairpin lace and crochet

Page 80

Tablecloth: Net darning, ladder cutwork, eyelet embroidery

Page 128

Large towels: tatting, macrame

Small towels: drawnwork mesh, cutwork

Page 134

Shelf edgings: Hardanger, tatting

Purses: netting, coronation cord with crochet

Yokes on undergarments: crochet, filet crochet

Dresses: machine-made lace